On Loving Men

On Loving Men

by
Jane Lazarre

The Dial Press   New York

Published by
The Dial Press
1 Dag Hammarskjold Plaza
New York, New York 10017

Manufactured in the United States of America
First printing

Design by Ann Gold

Library of Congress Cataloging in Publication Data
Lazarre, Jane.   On loving men.
    1. Men. 2. Lazarre, Jane. 3. Sex role.
4. Interracial marriage. 5. Interpersonal relations.
6. Love. I. Title.
HQ1090.L39   301.41   79-20812
ISBN 0-8037-6518-5

For my sons,
Adam and Khary

Acknowledgments

I would like to thank the people who helped me get through
the writing of this book.

Douglas H. White;
Carole Rosenthal and Lynda Schor, for their friendship
and their art;
Joyce Johnson, for her excellent and respectful criticism;
Wendy Weil, for help at the worst and best moments;
Martha Levin, for a lot of work and listening;
Pili Brache and Mirjam Billig, for coming into my life
when they did;
Jerry Raik, for helping me work when I could no longer look
at these pages;
Emily Lazarre, who is always there;
Eugene Straus, for his friendship;
and in stunned amazement at their constancy and deep gratitude
for their love and unending support, I thank Ruth Charney
Ross and Jane Monell Chase.

Contents

1
From Mother to Father

"What is required of her is a central shift of erotic allegiance . . ."

—Dorothy Dinnerstein,
The Mermaid and the Minotaur

Sometimes it seems to me that I have only two choices in life—to avoid my destiny, in which case I will use up great quantities of energy trying to fulfill someone else's concept of who I am, or to fulfill it. The trick is figuring out what my destiny is. Orphaned by the time I was in my early twenties, I was uncommonly free (or so I thought) to pursue my search. There was no one to hurt or to hide behind. No one standing in the wings shouting stage cues, predicting my mistakes with a deadly accuracy, pilfering for their own the golden heart of my triumphs. After many years of mourning my mother and my father, I became accustomed to thinking of my losses as accepted, my dead buried, my self an obedient mass of potential creation, lying there tamed and talented, waiting forever if need be for me to pick up my brush.

It is only in looking backward that one event can seem to have called forth the past, emblazoned the present moment with a meaning far deeper than itself, and ushered in a period of time during which familiar themes will be confronted again and again. That event seems to be the mark of some—if not final then at least crucial—turning point. I know, of course, that no such perfect causality exists. In the search for a beginning of a period in a life many elements must be considered—some capricious, some a matter of conscious choice. Still, looking backward a single event can seem the signal, the moment in which enormous changes began, as if everything funnels backward into that central image.

When my father-in-law died, my second child was only a few weeks away from being born. My own parents were dead. I was the pregnant mother of a three-year-old child, and my consciousness was firmly bounded by the protective and safe fusions of marriage. I sought security. I wanted the intense and somewhat unusual events of my childhood to remain safely past. My mother's long sickness and early death when I was seven; my father's complete involvement in the unpredictable and marginal life of an American Communist; my adolescence, which was filled with a sense of madness and chaos—these, I thought, could enrich my consciousness from a safe distance, suffusing my work and my mothering with a broad sense of human possibility, but they were over, the anxiety attached to them something merely remembered.

At my father-in-law's funeral I was conscious of an overwhelming desire to return to my past, to experience again the intense passions that my parents' deaths and lives had always evoked in me.

I have tried several times to paint the funeral procession, but I have failed. It is difficult for me to replicate the dignity I saw in the uniformity of color—black clothing, brown faces, black hair. Over and over again, for a mile it seemed to me, small pillars of this striped combination—black, brown, black. Behind them green of every shade, more browns, and blue. Once I left the sky out entirely, making figures so enormous that they covered the whole canvas, thinking it must be the human reflection of the regularities of nature that so moved me. Another time I painted most of the canvas blue, the vast sky around the southern farmland overtaking the mourners, their black, brown, and black reduced to suggestions, as if they were stems and branches not yet sprung out of the earth. Neither satisfied me. I have not been able to translate that feeling of emotional intensity bounded by ritual into paint. But perhaps it is not a technical problem. Often when I cannot surmount an apparently technical, artistic problem I discover it is a difficulty of another sort. There is some truth, usually a very simple one, pulling me away from an openness to work, that openness which is utterly necessary for the achievement of the precision that is eluding me. The sense of a pulling away from openness must be the block in concentration that people suffer, and each time I feel it I am reminded of the painting of the Indian woman in the pink shawl holding her baby, which hung on the wall of our living room when I was a child.

After my mother died, there were times when I suddenly felt the need to draw that painting. Grabbing my crayons, I would sit myself down on the rug in front of it and begin. I felt a need to rid myself of its image inside me, I think, and of the uncomfortable feeling of heat that came with it. At such times I would draw her well, the painting itself drawing her out of me onto my paper; once she was out, I would sit there, alone, cooled and relieved. But there were other times when I thought, If only I could learn to draw that pink shawl so that it looked exactly like the original, with the right light and shade, the right mixture of gray and rose, without the gray overtaking the rose so that it became a partially gray shawl instead of a pink one with shadows. Then I would sit down in front of my Indian woman, my pinks and grays spread before me, and whatever the reality of the shawl the picture as a whole would come out wrong. I would have this perfectly executed pink shawl, but then I would be at a loss as to how to fit the face within it.

Eventually I would begin having one of my famous tantrums, enraging my father who would send me to my room shouting after me, "Why do you always draw that damn painting? Try something else. What do you see there? Draw castles. Draw some nice flowers. Or fruit. Draw fruit."

I would sit on the bed then, breathing heavily with fury, clenching my teeth, staring murderously at the slammed door where I knew he would appear at any moment. When he sent me to my room he could never leave me there to cool off, but instead always followed me, continuing his tirade, his cheeks turning red, his finger pointing dramatically at the ceiling, his analysis of my temperamental failings punctuated by criticisms of my more mundane habits, and all without pause pouring eloquently out of his mouth: "And furthermore is it necessary always to draw? Night after night after night? It's not right. You listen to me . . . don't bite your nails. Your mother had beautiful nails. Manicured. Life is not a continuous moment of emotional excitement."

With the word *continuous* he would raise his voice. With the word *excitement* he would spread his hands wide and tense his fingers so that each seemed to stand out as a

separate lightning bolt from the palms of his hands, and I
grew to imagine there was a tightrope suspended between
them which a tiny version of me was walking.

"In between there must be times of careful thought,"
he'd continue. "Take your hair out of your eyes—I could
swear you had a forehead when you were born—you
can't just race into the living room and throw your crayons on the ground and begin to draw. You have to be
careful. Controlled."

He was afraid that I would burn myself up before I
was twenty, as though my emotional life were a rather
short candle. Having expressed his fear, he would heave a
great sigh, and, sitting down on the bed near me, he'd pat
my shoulder or my thigh while I, feeling wronged and
unaided but sounding resigned, would say, "Oh, I just
won't draw her anymore," knowing I could never explain
to him about the heat she made me feel, and the cooling
afterward. For weeks I would draw the orange fruit and
the blue flowers that my father desired.

After three long and difficult tries, I have put my
painting of the funeral in the closet. By now it is an un-
differentiated mass of blacks and browns with a few points
at which a rather muddy blue peeks through the layers of
darker paint. I cannot translate the meaning of that day
down south when we buried William into visual image.
But I know that it was one of those experiences which in
retrospect lies as a static point in time, between a beginning and an end, at once symbolizing the nature of my
past and warning me of a future whose inevitable truths I
was trying very hard to deny.

It was mid-August in North Carolina and I had
never been so hot. It was a breathless air without the New

York dampness, and, without that tangible humidity to attach myself to, I felt as if I was in an unearthly place—a place so still and stylized, it was more like a film I was watching than life itself. There was a sense of vision, but touch was gone. I sweated heavily as we were directed to the living room of William's sister's farmhouse. We had to form a double line, our successive places determined by the degree of our relation to the widow. She naturally led the procession, on her youngest son's arm. Behind them was the eldest, William junior and his family. Then my husband, James; my son; and myself. Behind us the sisters, brothers, aunts, uncles, and various more distantly related kin. There were about twenty of us, every single person in black, total black, except for the children, who wore white and blue.

The immediate family in this straight double line followed the director of the funeral home (an old family friend and clearly a man of authority) out the door, and then under the vast blue sky I saw that seemingly infinite line of black-clad mourners waiting for us to enter the cars so that they might follow in theirs. Black, brown, and black moved across the green toward us, but didn't quite touch the deepest mourners, the most bereaved, the next of kin. They just moved slightly toward us like a striped wave and pulled away again, making room, sighing in pity. Following the widow's example, we maintained a quiet dignity. This was a Catholic family, and that implied a certain decorum.

I may have seemed startled, I hope imperceptibly, when the striped waves moved toward me. I had never before been a part of such ordered ritual, an elegant structure of color and controlled movement in which Death, I feared, might almost slip away unnoticed.

In celebrations of death, I was accustomed to confusion, hysteria, aimless wandering—the more confused, aimless, and wandering the hysteria, the greater the love was the belief. And if you were not dressed in a perceptibly sloppy manner, with at least one clashing color, then it meant you had been far too attentive to appearances when you ought to have been focused entirely upon the contemplation of your loss.

Now I thanked whatever gods were in the hot air around us, Mary and Jesus, I supposed, that I had given in to my mother-in-law and gone shopping for a proper dress.

"What's the difference what you wear?" I had complained, perturbed at the many discussions concerning the outfitting of every member of the family, impatient with what struck me as a diversion from the horrible fact which had come clear the past Saturday morning after a night of slow waiting outside the Intensive Care Unit of the hospital.

We waited all night for him to rally, but at six the tired doctor released us from our vigil, stating in an oddly matter-of-fact way, "Well, he's dead."

Then we had to wait for them to pull out all the tubes which had failed to revive him so that the family could go in and say good-bye. I let them go without me. I walked toward the room, peeked in at Death like a child frightened of recrimination, and then made a fast retreat. I could do without all those revived memories of mine, I told myself then. I'd cry for William. I didn't have to see him dead. Death has a way of taking everyone in when you see it up close. I had no desire to see my father, or my mother—Sylvia—peering at me through William's closed face.

It had seemed a sacrilege to my atheistic sensibility

to worry about clothes. Nevertheless, my mother-in-law, Marie, and I had done a careful shopping, pushing through all the black dresses on the rack, comparing notes about subtle signs of sophistication or appropriateness, discovering in a line or a stitch the clear mark of *class* which William would have wanted upon us: a badge.

"That's it," Marie said with regal certainty the moment she saw me in the one with the Mexican lace on the collar and cuffs.

Now as I stood holding James's hand, my feet, swollen from heat and pregnancy, stuffed into proper black pumps, waiting my turn to turn to enter the car which would ride first behind the hearse, I shuddered at the thought of being not only the only white person in the funeral procession but, if I hadn't listened to Marie, the only person except for the children not wearing black. Instead, I radiated appropriateness, my Mexican lace collar falling gracefully across my chest, my black mantilla lying modestly upon my oddly straight hair.

In the car we could relax a bit. We let our son play musical chairs with his cousin on the little seats that unfolded in front of us like the ones in Checker cabs. Even Marie smiled as her grandson, uncommonly formal in his starched blue and white suit, demanded his ratty old pacifier as desperately as some of the grownups were reaching for cigarettes. He suctioned it into his mouth and relaxed. Someone straightened my mantilla. James, always sociable, asked the driver questions about his business.

As we came off the country road and turned onto the main thoroughfare of the black part of town, people stopped and stood respectfully still until, I supposed, the entire funeral train had passed. The men took off their hats and held them with both hands in front of them. The women nodded their heads, murmuring.

William had been baptized a Catholic only ten minutes before he died, his slate wiped clean, and whatever the nature of the sins that had kept him from conversion all those years, they were, I presume, forgiven, and when we arrived at the church the priest stepped out to meet him.

I am anxious sitting in this small, simple church, having irrationally imagined the ornate cathedrals I have knelt in on Fifth Avenue and remembering one in Italy where I spent many hours staring at the curving stone and dark crevices of the robe of Michelangelo's Moses. I wanted to rest my body against his cold marble folds.

But this little church is finite and manageable. The mourners are neither crying nor screaming. They listen quietly as the priest, who did not know William, pieces together a eulogy of his virtues, unmatched pieces of a puzzle from old friends that remain disconnected, meaningless, and unfamiliar. I love funerals. They are an unmasking of pretense. Death is recognized as the unavoidable presence I have always felt it to be. And, unlike a personal confrontation with a dead body, there is ritual to form a subtle but forceful boundary line, a way of enclosing and permitting excess. My father feared excess, but at certain funerals it was allowed.

With this clash of expectation and muted, dull reality my anxiety grows. I am waiting, but no one wails deeply and loud. I realize shamelessly that I have been looking forward to this day, to the opportunity for the loud guttural sounds to explode, creating an instantaneous, if momentary, relief from life pain. If the instant could be preserved, that low moaning instant . . . what is it in the feel of the sound that so relieves?

I had actually wanted to meet my father here. Or Sylvia.

I begin to say *Sylvia* out loud, my whispers camouflaged by the prayer-singing. Funerals are one of the few places where I still dare to seek Sylvia. Otherwise, I have learned to let her rest in peace. But I am determined to allow this thing that happens to me at funerals to happen —the burning of old losses, the retrieving of the distant as well as the recent past. Perhaps I must periodically invite the dangerous past in like this so that later I will possess all the more a sense of my own survival.

My mother and father divided their children between them. I was my mother's. My sister was my father's. When Sylvia died I had no intention of letting her go. After the funeral period was over, her picture began to appear everywhere in the house. In the living room there was a portrait painted by her sister, composed almost entirely of shades of dark green. The black pupils were set precisely in the middle of the eyes so that no matter where you walked in the room, the eyes seemed to look at you, and as they did the expression of the face, particularly around the mouth, would begin to change. Believing that Death was a place and could as well be in the white walls directly behind the dark green portrait as anywhere, I'd walk back and forth in the room, peering at the painted face, talking conversationally with my mother about the events of the day. Then, as though I had cranked up an old-fashioned automobile, gotten it ready, I would sit down for a while and hold on to the put-put-put of the engine, the moment of consciousness, of the world arranged in a way which was comprehensible. Afterward, the uncomfortable feeling of heat would diminish for a while and I would feel as if a beautifully patterned mass of crystalline ice moved within me, covering everything, quieting intensity into an exquisite stillness.

That was my secret relationship with the dark green portrait. The old, black-and-white photograph which they had hung in my room demanded a more rigorous sort of ritual. Each night in the dark after the grownups had retreated to the living room, I had to stand up on my bed and walk slowly toward the picture. Holding each side of the black frame in my hands, I would lean over and kiss the glass three times. This proved my filial devotion, it was my oath never to forget. If I slept away from home, which I rarely did, as soon as the lights were turned out I would concentrate with all my might, eyes closed against appearances, on the photograph of my mother. With sufficient concentration I could conjure up the image with such a sense of reality that all other thoughts were banished from my mind. My energy focused thus, I was ready to kiss the smiling face in my mind with as much conviction as if she were actually there.

It was then I began to believe in the reality of the inner world, to stop distinguishing as others seemed to between external and internal life, always estimating which contained greater quantities of "reality"—as if reality were a liquid that could be poured and measured and existed only when visible in a glass vial. And I learned at times to be able to focus my energy with a strict discipline, like a spotlight gathering all the little spots of light into one funnel, pointed inward to see what was there. Or I grew to believe this was how I attained that facility which would come and go through the years. But perhaps I was wrong. Perhaps I had been born with it. Or perhaps I only thought I viewed reality, but what I was actually seeing was merely one more dark green portrait, someone's (my own?) vision of what the world might be like if someone decided suddenly to create it.

Or maybe I had not learned it from my mother, but from my father, who was all I was left with now that Sylvia, at least in most respects, was gone.

There would be times when I'd think I was more like my father than my mother, that that was the reason for his dislike. There would be times when I would so emphasize this identification with my father that I would forget how much Sylvia had meant to me, forget sitting in the bath after she had stepped out and watching as she dried her body with a large towel, holding it in both hands and pulling it gently across her back until the little rivers were gone and only a wide tan softness remained; forget how with mouth slightly opened in fascination I had watched her put a thin white elastic around her waist and attach a clean white pad of cotton to each end, resting the wide middle part softly under her vagina, then covering her whole body with a long, pink robe. After brushing her black hair she would lean over into the water to gather me up in another soft towel and carry me into my bedroom, warm except for the thin line of wet coolness around my hairline where the washcloth had dampened my bangs.

With her death, things that might have been remembered were forgotten, as well as the other way around. For example, I could not remember, after several years, the sound of Sylvia's voice or the feel of a woman's body holding me, and I came to expect dark, nighttime, intimate face rubs from faces with rough beards on them. The feel of a straight flat chest was to me the meaning of protection and nurturance, and the feel of breasts against my cheek soon became a frightening thing, one which threatened to call forth in all its enormity what I had been deprived of.

On the other hand, I could not forget that afternoon in my aunt's house making up a play with my cousins. Just before curtain time, my aunt came into the room and asked that I accompany her to a neighbor's apartment. I looked so cute in my black leotard and tights, she said, that someone wanted to take my picture. I was playing a black horse in the play, a horse for a princess who was played by my cousin, and I would gallop across the stage for the parents, gallop into the wind shaking my wild thoughts loose and freeing my already frequently cluttered mind from my already much-too-real fantasies. Running like that, from the living room into the far end of the dining room and back, there would be no thoughts, only air to move through and the feel of slipping wood under my heels. So, rehearsing, I galloped down the hall to meet the photographer. But only my father waited in the neighbor's apartment.

He sat quite still on the couch, sad looking, drawn, even to a small child's eyes, bereft.

And so I knew. My mother's dead, I thought, and said, "What's the matter?"

"Come here, baby," he said, holding out arms which with weakness had lost their familiar suggestion of security.

I was afraid of my father. Afraid of his sadness. Of his loss. That he would cry.

And he did. He did cry. Loud and long with deep moans and more and more tears as he looked at me calling my name again and again. Then all his moans moved from English into Yiddish, turning from Oh, God into *oy, oy, oy*, and that made it worse. The irrationality of it, the incomprehensibility of it stunned me as he threatened to turn before my eyes into my grandmother who could not even read English. Then I started to laugh. But held it in in time. No one would ever know how I had almost laughed when he finally gasped, "Mommy's dead. She's not coming back anymore."

I reached my hand over my mouth to hide the criminal smile and gasped, refusing to believe what I had known for days had been true. I knew I had been sleeping at my aunt's for three days of funeral preparations, and I had known the day of the funeral itself when my aunt and uncle left in the morning crying.

I had asked them, "Is Mommy going to die?" And instead of *No, darling*, which they had said during the three years of her sickness, they had said, *We don't know*. It was enough of a change to signal. And this kind postponement the grownups were trying to provide would forever seem to me a horrifying betrayal, a pointless and cruel lie.

Now, terrified of my crying father reaching out for my black-horse body, I reached out for my aunt who was crying too, but was at least not moaning in Yiddish and who smelled like her sister, my mother, when she was angry and when she laughed.

The black horse, created for galloping, sister of the wind, curled there, and with big, staring eyes, watched my father try to gain control. As his breathing evened he reached out again, knowing he had frightened me, and I went to him, the man who had always been so strange to me; whose lap was across the green-rug sea from home on

Sylvia's; whose arms were the place called Russia on the globe, where he had been born, whose accents he still possessed, whose land was unfamiliar and desired and into whose warmth I nestled as an adventure, but not as a nightly reunion with myself. Now Russia would be all I had. I held him and hugged him, saying Mommy's dead, wondering if it could indeed be true—this absurdity, this outrage, this unbelievable abandonment. Never again. Never never again.

When he began to moan again I was taken away. The play was canceled. They told the others.

For a while I disbelieved. I was taking a bath with my older cousin who said with an impish grin, "You know your mother didn't really die yesterday."

Of course, the black horse thought, of course, these odd people have fooled me. What a thing to do—to make up such impossible stories. And the horse, heaving a sigh of relief, reared.

But my cousin, moving clear shiny bubbles across the rivers between the soap mountains, said, "She really died Thursday."

And there were undeniable facts. Sylvia's clothes were gone. Her songs were gone. Her blue box of white napkins under the bathroom sink was gone. Secrets came to take their place. The secret of the eyes in the dark green portrait which shortly after the death I began to draw each night. When they insisted that I stop, fearing morbidity, I turned toward the Indian woman in the pink shawl holding her dark little boy which hung on the opposite wall. There were masks and disguises enough if one were forbidden to embrace the real thing. I found more and more secrets as I grew, the place called Death, for example, which opened up green and brown and welcoming behind the photograph.

Only in the middle of the night when I screamed *I want her* and she didn't come, not ever again, did I question the reality of my secrets. Then, wrenched from the woman, dark giant mirror of myself, I began to look over to the other side of the house at the blue-eyed man whom I had to learn to love and force into loving me back.

Or had he always loved me, just been afraid of the child who, despite her looks, reminded him of himself and of his secretive, passionate, and somewhat overwhelming family?

Sylvia had been strong, in control of her emotions and her possessions, keeping the drawers of her desk neatly ordered—one for envelopes, one for paper, one for pressed white handkerchiefs with borders of violets or red hearts or silvery embroidery. But the house which had been beautiful and elegant began to grow tattered. Incompleteness was everywhere. Unreplaced silverware sets so that no one could ever find more than three knives no matter who came to dinner; unmended chair covers; empty closets where her clothes had been that went unfilled for years. My room and my sister's, decorated in pink ruffles and chintz, grew tan and black over time, and I, black horse seeking its mirror, learned to prefer it that way. He pressured me always to become like her—dignified and elegant. But I sometimes suspected that I was (had become?) more like him.

Each night I kissed the picture. Regularly I drew the Indian mother. Each year, on the death-date anniversary, I pretended it was that year again and recorded the events in my diary as if it were then, trying to make it sound as immediate as possible. Reading my childish diary twenty years later, I would find the same afternoon recorded over and over in handwriting that matured and changed with each year, only the handwriting attesting to the fact that time had passed, that one moment had not lasted forever.

Sitting in the small, stark southern church, I look downward, at the prayerbook, at the wooden ledge for kneeling, anywhere so long as I can continue looking inward, recapturing in the strange orderliness of this ritual of death the most intense moments of my past.

"He was a devoted father," says the priest, and I relinquish my eyes to the altar. I count the yellows in the stained glass. Humble for a minute, I let my ghosts rest.

"Parental love," says the childless priest, "is the most utterly Christian sort of love in the living universe. Our children's sorrows are our own. Their joys and triumphs are welcomed without envy, in deep fulfillment. In a sense there is no separation between our children and ourselves."

My son, only moderately distractible at three and only half Christian, whines and begins tearing a prayerbook. As the congregation with one face glances at my child, I fulfill the priest's description, feeling it is I who have whined.

"His pacifier," I snarl at James, as the time for communion is announced. But my son wiggles his face away from the rubber plug and will not be silenced. I hold him against me, letting him peer over my shoulder, and this stops his restlessness for a moment. I wonder if the congregation remarks quietly at the slightly intrusive display between a white mother and her black child. In the old days, I would have wished for a more color-blind kind of relation, but by now I know this to be impossible. My whiteness shines like an annoying streetlight which doesn't get turned off even after midnight, and it always will.

As everyone begins to file past me to take communion I am thankful to have my son in my arms, and I pat his back, shove the pacifier in, jostle him as I did when he was an infant, hoping to induce in him a serenity which has never once been evident in his fiery nature.

Finally people begin to rise, file out behind the pallbearers, get back in their cars for the drive out to the cemetery. In 1973 there is one interracial cemetery in town, and there has been some question as to where William ought to be buried. If he is laid to rest in the primarily white cemetery, his body will spend eternity in well-tended, beautiful surroundings. Furthermore, the black cemetery is on a hill and if there are floods, the grounds have been known to become so muddy that the graves open and the coffins float to the surface. Still, there he will be among his own, and that finally has been the deciding factor.

At the gravesite a canopy to protect the mourners from the sun awaits us. We fold in under it, encircling the departed to say goodbye. Marie, her arms full of tall, red roses, kneels beside the coffin. She straightens the leaves surrounding one of the many bouquets. She pulls out a white card of sympathy attached to another so that all of the bereaved will be equally noticed. She is an attentive housewife, straightening, fixing, as though preparing a child for a party, adjusting a collar, smoothing a curl. Several nights before, I had watched in amazement as she ironed William's outfit for the burial—the suit, the shirt, the matching tie—her final wifely duty. This concentration on the mundane strikes me as funny in a way, but also draws my respect as an acceptance of the pain in life, rather than a rebellion against it, always does.

"What's that?" shouts my son pointing to the large box in which his grandfather lies. People smile tolerantly and James whispers, "That's Grandpa. That's where he will rest from now on." He carefully avoids mentioning the fact that the box will be placed underground, fending off insomnia and night terrors, possible reactions of a child to death which I have tried to describe to James in precise detail, warning him close to fifty times not to dare mention the underground part.

"Then they put him in the ground," says our son, and James smiles in a self-satisfied manner.

I am struck again by James's enviable sense of his own separateness. Here he is at his father's funeral and he sits at the gravesite, part of him mourning, crying, concerned about his mother, and yet a part of him sits untouched. *I am James*, says the separate part, *I am not in a coffin, not dead, not a little boy losing a parent but a fairly self-reliant adult experiencing one of the inevitabilities of human life.*

I want to feel that way instead of always on the point of some new, dangerous merging. My love is coated with envy and I think: Wait until he sees. Next week. Next month. He will lose control. I anticipate those moments when he will lean against me and I will hold him, pull his cheek down onto my breast, help him.

But James will never relinquish to me his protective distance, and, while I wait for him to falter, that cooling stream of objectivity seems to spread and lighten his limbs, its undeniable function not to mock me but to support himself.

I remember wanting to lose my boundaries at William's grave. I conjured up my sorrows like a witch fixing a carefully balanced magical brew which would become the atmosphere for the spirit's dance. While the priest chanted Latin phrases, I translated silently into Yiddish, familiar keynotes to any emotional extreme—death, birth, fury, passion. My old aunt who came to this country when she was four, and who always spoke English, called in Yiddish for her husband to return to her the day we buried him, and in Yiddish she threatened to jump into his open grave.

I remember that a delighted smile threatened to break through as I welcomed my fantastic band of risen spirits dancing down the narrow aisles, until at last the more recent death, my own father's, announced itself. After all, the coffin held a father. If James would not feel anguish at the loss, even if in fact he never felt that absolute paternal protection, then I would feel it for him. In that moment I didn't care in how many ways my father had disapproved of me, nor did I care to recall the times, after Sylvia's death, when he tried so obviously and so painfully to make me his own.

I had worked myself up to this point, I see now. I had recalled the intricacies of my mother's death, which I had relived so often, understood so carefully, until I had finally seen that no amount of understanding would ever diminish the loss. I had recalled the familiar pain so that I could come to the newer death prepared. My father had been dead for five years. I had cried, dreamed, mythologized, written of his death. But the intricacies of his legacy had been forgotten in my attempt to bury my need of him.

It is fatherhood I am willing to remember now. One mourns what one has not yet relinquished. I cried not only for William whose death, at fifty, was premature, but for a confident, aloof, and invulnerable manhood whose death, though perhaps long overdue, was not yet achieved. It was the loss of that wonderful, tyrannical conviction against which I had always measured myself that I was ready to feel again and to mourn.

2
Father and Daughter

For no one attracted her more; his hands were beautiful, and his feet, and his voice, and his words, and his haste, and his temper, and his oddity, and his passion, and his saying straight out before every one, we perish, each alone, and his remoteness. (He had opened his book.) But what remained intolerable, she thought, sitting upright, and watching Macalister's boy tug the hook out of the gills of another fish, was that crass blindness and tyranny of his which had poisoned her childhood and raised bitter storms, so that even now she woke in the night trembling with rage and remembered some command of his; some insolence: "Do this," "Do that," his dominance: his "Submit to me."

—Virginia Woolf,
To the Lighthouse

My passion for my father grew out of my mother's death. It was a passion that was born of a fear of his continued rejection, fired by a desire to find and develop some connection between us, nurtured by the very real similarities between us in our temperaments and in our thought. My sister, who resembled his fair-haired and blue-eyed family, possessed that envied paternal adoration— she was her father's little girl. But I slowly discovered that there was a way in which I could claim his attention—through my willingness to inherit his ideas and his theories, and through my ability, which I had surely inherited from him, to put thought into words.

The intellectual metaphor of my father's passion was Marxism. While the Marxist theory of history and the economic relations of society deepened his compassion and gave a rational analysis to his great personal sense of the injustices of poverty and prejudice, he had a dangerously romantic tendency to discover heroes wherever he went. After all, in the making and changing of history, there was an unavoidable need for the exceptional individual.

When my mother died I saw that to earn his love I would have to become one of those heroes. By the time a few years had passed, being a hero had come to seem the only way to be anything at all.

I began to succeed in certain ways. And yet a tension between us would always remain, a feeling that I was essentially unacceptable, a constant suspicion that I was failing him. When the Sunday discussions on Marxism and Leninism were done, I always felt that, whatever tests I had passed, there were others, more sinister and far less appropriate to out-loud discussion, in which I always fell just short of victory.

When he reviewed *The Story of a Real Man*, the most recent Soviet novel he had read, retelling the story with carefully chosen words spiced here and there with an exotic vowel sound of his native Russian, I passed every test of comprehension at the end, reciting the lesson that "real" manhood had more to do with quiet courage than with brute force. Under his careful tutoring, I began to sense the dangers of left-wing communism as an infantile disorder; and, around the age of twelve, I began to grasp the importance of economics as a force in history. Still, my glory in his approval was always short-lasting. No sooner would he begin to express his pride in my achievements to various friends and relations, than Mr. Nash, the superintendent, would find me on the roof again, petting with some boy.

My father saw these two parts of me as thesis and antithesis on the Question of Dignity. Reasonable self-control took its place in opposition to self-revelation, but it took me some time to become fully conscious of the contradiction.

I knew only that I had failed him. It was an uncontrollable kind of failure—something that had to do with the way my skin tended to break out when I first began menstruating; the way I liked to sit with my legs apart; the fact that I hated high-heeled shoes because of my weak ankles; and my inescapable surrender to that rhythmic beating in my vagina which could be called forth so easily by some boy's hand or by my own.

I remember that my sister once told me of the time she was sitting on a country lawn, her legs spread wide apart as she picked clover, chewed grass, gazed inward, I imagine, with the help of the sun-heat on her eyelids. My father, noticing her there, called her to a *conference*, his word for a serious talk regarding critical failures of expectation—parental, social, or otherwise. The conference was, again, on Dignity. Her small, soft vagina, pink and white as the inside of a conch, had been showing.

This memory is the twin of one of mine. The one about my father's best friend—a man so close to my father that, despite their differences, I often find myself confusing his memory with my father's, dreaming of one when I mean the other. (Now that they are dead, distinctions fade. They both lectured on Marx, kissed wet kisses, tried to love their daughters as they would sons.) Yet I distinctly remember hearing him snicker like a schoolboy behind a nasty hand, and to a man who was a complete stranger to me, about the early and full development of my breasts.

It is not that my father was uncritical of my intellect. Although he generally approved of my development in this regard, there were certain unmistakable characteristics of that other part of my nature which had a tendency to creep into my studies as well. These were: overintensity, impatience, and a sloppy attitude. Just as each time I went shopping for a pink, pin-striped summer dress and matching white pumps, I somehow returned from Ohrbach's with black ballet shoes which my father considered slutty and another brown or green polo shirt to add to my already undeniably adequate collection; just as each time I broke up with a boy and swore to "play the field," I would almost immediately become involved again in going steady so I could rush up to the roof where Mr. Nash would always miraculously find me; just as when I was supposed to be practicing piano lessons so that Mrs. MacVicky would choose me to perform in the next children's concert, I would find myself uncontrollably drawn to the Fairy-Giant game in which the deep notes were the giants and the high notes were the fairies and they would chase each other all over the keys, ceasing only when the Goddess of Night appeared on the black keys, asserting, with the assistance of the bass pedal, her authority and majesty; just as all these were true, it was also true that I had a tendency to defend an uncompromising political position without enough facts to back me up; that I refused to learn that firsts came first in matters of intellect and one cannot proceed to the interesting final chapters without mastering the basics; and that I had trouble keeping categories separate.

In my seventh-grade math class I was asked to compare two textbooks we were using and to prepare a paragraph of criticism. I liked the newer one better because the diagrams were blue and yellow, the topic sentences were red, and there were even certain equations in which colors burst like a sudden circular rainbow all over the unknown x as it was shown to be equal to the unknown y. My outraged math teacher read my paper to the class, identifying it only as obviously the essay of a female: "She likes the colors better," he said sarcastically, and all the class, including my cowardly and mortified self, laughed uproariously at the unnamed, stupid girl.

I ran home to tell my father, remembering his repeated instructions about the dignity of standing alone in the face of humiliation if you are certain you are right. I found sympathy for my tears and humiliation, but then he had to wonder how I could in fact have answered the assignment in such a way. Didn't I realize that Mr. Stringboch was asking about *math*?

In Marxism, I was most attracted to the idea of the Fetishism of Commodities—that wonderful theory about the way our objectifications of the material goods of our lives turn around on us like little arrow-boomerangs, transforming our feelings, even our *thoughts*, our concepts of knowledge itself, into objects no more magical or valued or authentic than the chair in the corner or the coat on our backs.

"Even our concept of knowledge itself!" I used to scream at him. "Dad, do you see what that means?!"

Once I grasped Fetishism of Commodities, I lost all interest in Surplus Value, dreaming sloppily as my father intoned his lecture on Art as Superstructure, just the sort of topic which was now certain to release only boredom in me. More and more often I sought the roof and those boyish thighs and fingers which felt so hard and soft and good to me.

Or perhaps it was only that I was getting nearer sixteen than twelve and my attention had begun to waver. By then I was certain that the mysterious, deepest part of me was somehow wrong to my father, and I began to keep careful inner records of my failures. Even now, each time I fall short of some abstract expectation, I hear his softly accented voice helping me keep accurate count.

The saddest and most infuriating part of this is that with passing years, and related experience, his voice tends to broaden, fed by others more vicious than his own. This conglomerate voice never seems to tire of nesting critically in my ear until, sooner or later, I have to speak out loud to it: Quiet now! I say, I don't want to hear you. Thus I acknowledge its reality, for denial only makes it louder, as though it were coming through a foghorn. But at the same time, I assert control. With repetition of that sentence, *Quiet now* (am I implying that at some later time, I will listen, buying time with false promises?), I practice self-control. Respect for a self that exists away from the paternal voice. I search for that old self in my love for women. Through them I try to love men differently. What I can do easily with women is exactly what I have come to fear most with fathers, brothers, lovers, and even sons at times: to utterly reveal myself.

But repeatedly I ask myself: what is the name of this unacceptable, potentially devouring core?

In my teenage years, I read over and over again about the mythological heroic quest. The young man, determined to discover the meaning of life, willingly sacrifices material comfort, even risks death, in order to descend into the underworld, where he will meet monsters and tricksters of all sorts; where he will be tested repeatedly; where he can discover, if he is courageous and intelligent enough, the secret of life. This secret of life is never sought merely for personal aggrandizement, nor is its function, once grasped, to benefit the individual alone. Rather, it is a gift to the world. Whether or not the People accept the gift, won at such great risk and price, nevertheless, it is for them, and if they reject it now, then some day—even if it is centuries later—they will understand its worth, its eternal symbolic importance, as well as the supreme dedication of the hero, a dedication born not of idealistic self-sacrifice, but of deeply felt personal anguish.

In his many travels, through the literature, paintings, and sculpture which inspired my childish imagination, the hero was inevitably forced to leave loved ones (women) behind; a woman was always waving goodbye from some shore, giving him up for dead while she mourned within some castle, birthing another son who would be beautiful and kind but who could never take the place of the hero.

When the hero returned, his mother (wife) would be waiting for him. Years had passed. Presumably, she had lived a life. But at the moment of return, it was as if she had not lived at all, as if between the two moments of his departure and his return, she had treaded emotional water, ceased, virtually, to exist at all.

The twentieth-century heroes struggled against gods of a different sort. Joseph K. fought indictments from unidentifiable authorities; Meursault, victim of a supreme alienation, fell into a profound doubt of the meaning and worth of life itself; Stephen Dedalus took his stand on the side of artistic expression with its investigation of the deepest layers of the self, facing down cultural tradition both in content—the bigoted and limited Irish Catholicism of his origins—and also in form—the insistence that sentences conform to an ancient concept of completion, and that thought follow thought in a thoroughly reasonable, conscious and one-dimensional way. But I was no less involved with their quest for the delineation of the self from the background of the universe, no less identified with their anguish than I had been with the more morally consistent heroes of ancient myth. I imagine them all in a symbolic circle surrounding Michelangelo's prisoners, which had moved me deeply for reasons that at the time were unclear. Whether poetic or sculpted, ancient or modern, each hero was struggling to be born from the uniformity of stultifying stone in which he was everlastingly embedded. The maleness of these heroes seemed incidental to me. They represented issues which had plagued me since I could remember being conscious of death.

It was late at night and I was tossing and turning with anxiety, victim of a chronic insomnia. Suddenly I realized—in a moment as many children do—that as my mother had died, I would die too, and what immediately came into blazing consciousness were those unavoidable, awful questions: what was the meaning of my life? the significance of my actions? What, I thought (although not in such terms—having no idea of the long and respectable history of my sudden doubts), was the efficacy of morality itself?

It was always with that moment in mind that I forced my imagination into heroic adventure after adventure. I abandoned Snow White, Sleeping Beauty, and the rest with their retreat into the domesticity offered them by their vapid princes, and I threw in my lot with Ulysses, with Captain Ahab, even with Jesus. These were the living symbols of my enormous inner ambivalence. I poured my fears and my losses, my arrogance and my strength, into their beings, and I followed along.

My vulnerability to the appeal of heroes was ensured through the years not only by my father's romantic vision of world history, but by his own history as well. When he was a young boy, living in the city of Kishinev, then Rumania, behind the tea room from which his father derived a modest living, he became involved with the ideas of the Communists. His life as a boy seemed to move forward between a series of brutal paternal beatings, their devastating psychological effect mitigated only by the protection—when she was not afraid—of his mother, and the nightly embraces and cuddlings of his toothless, old grandmother with whom he shared a bed. In school, he was once more subject to cruel and indiscriminate beatings by grown men, the schoolmasters, who were trying to force his rebellious mind, which was by nature attracted to the concrete, to the inductive, artistic point of view, into that aspect of the scholarly Hebrew tradition which is committed to reason, to intellectual authoritarianism, to abstract consistent rules deduced from unquestioned, historically formulated principles. No room for the hero and his quest in those classrooms, not for a sensitive and in-

quisitive boy (his father called him feminine) like my
father.

Later my father would insist, contrary to all convention, that he wanted daughters and not sons. My mother
must have breathed a sigh of relief when she brought him
two girls. But his father, fortunately, never lived long
enough to witness his son's continuing development in
precisely the direction he had most feared: my father
hated sports, showed no interest in material profit, insisted
that his daughters "learn a trade" and avoid domestic en-
slavement to an autocratic husband.

Still in Kishinev at the age of fifteen, my father was
very involved with the political work of the Communist
Party. But his older sisters began moving, one by one, to
the United States. Then an older brother followed them.
Finally he, as the only remaining son, had to emigrate as
well and so accompany his parents to their eldest children,
who had established themselves in the then Jewish neighborhood of Strawberry Mansion on the north side of Phil-
adelphia. His first action was to join the American
Communist Party, remaining an active member, frequently in a leadership capacity, for the next forty-five
years. Throughout the world he went: to Spain, to East
Germany, to Moscow—to American prisons—defying the
monsters of capitalism, of greed, of bigotry. Secretly I
merged his quest with that of Odysseus; and to my adoles-
cent mind Don Quixote was neither madman nor artist,
but a full-time functionary of the Communist Party who
had gone underground.

Whatever my father found in the sixty-eight years he
lived, whatever treasures he returned to the people, whatever false prizes lured him, deflecting his energy temporarily from his true quest, it was his search, and not its

outcome, that inspired my chronically unsatisfied and always too uncompromising character. It is his dedication, his consistent dedication, to his quest for truth that continues to inspire me today.

I cannot remember the point in my reading, imagining, and pretending when I suddenly realized that the hero was always a boy, that I had read of no father nurturing the passion for the search in the heart of a girl, bestowing the burden of discovery upon the shoulders of a daughter. But taking courage and a certain amount of necessary hubris from the fact that my father, unlike most others I knew, had actually wanted daughters and did not see us as substitutes for the boys he never had, I responded to this sudden awareness with rage rather than humility. I remember feeling this rage when I read Paul Goodman's *Growing Up Absurd*, which all of my friends were then reading. But in that work two streams of intellectual and political consciousness come together: one: that human beings live enmeshed in psychic and universal oppositions whose only possible reconciliation lies in deepening consciousness—a kind of revolutionary mixture of acceptance and rebellion; and two: that the lives of women cannot symbolize this consciousness of eternal and natural oppositions, nor do women feel driven to make their tangled way through them, seeking understanding of the self and justice for the people, because, simply, women can and do give birth.

And finally Joseph K., Meursault, even Stephen Dedalus, stood apart from me as they never had before, stood threateningly apart, clothed mockingly in all their maleness, just as if they had been the boys in the park who allowed us to play ball with them only at their discretion, and who otherwise preferred us sitting on the fence, watching them, tugging at our straight skirts which were always rising a bit too revealingly above the knee.

At the age of sixteen, when I first read these books, I can recall absolutely no desire to give birth. Babies and the idea of having them were as foreign to me as they might have been to my cousin Max, whose temperamental inclination to quest-seeking was respected not only by our somewhat philosophical family, but by the world around us as well. It was also in my sixteenth year that I was educated with excruciating care on the subject of birth control, and then marched by a loved older woman into the office of her friend, the gynecologist, for a diaphragm fitting. I received my instructions in the magical techniques of avoiding conception very seriously, as any hero, her eyes set on the cavernous mazes and labyrinths of the underworld, should. And at the age of twenty-six, when I did find myself pregnant for the first time in my life, it was a startling revelation to me. My view of myself was drastically altered and threatened. I had a sense of having been transformed suddenly into an unfamiliar form of life, a modern equivalent of the princes who were always being turned into frogs and bears. It requires continual effort to integrate this *mother-self* into the Wandering Hero, there being, to say the least, very little social permission to fulfill my maternal obligations in personally creative rather than externally imposed forms. In this struggle, I am frequently reminded of my father's youthful attempts to protect his unconforming turn of mind from his Hebrew teacher, forced to rebel not as a result of some consciously derived principle of justice or the dignity of the self, but because, given who he was, he could not do otherwise. In early motherhood I discovered that my being would not conform to the conventional demands of American femininity. I missed my heroes who must by now, I feared, have continued their quest without me, thinking I had been devoured somewhere along the treacherous way.

The young girl who was outraged to be so summarily excluded from the search she had after many years come to envision as her own, was the only self I knew. Knowingly or not, my father had broken the rule of the son's exclusive right to the obligations of the search, and insisted that I accept the challenge. This challenge, I think now, is the greatest gift a father can bestow upon a daughter.

Then what in fact was the unacceptable core?

I continue to believe that my father was not disappointed that I wasn't a son. There was, on the contrary, something about my being a daughter that inspired him, that allowed him to identify with my spiritual growth in a way which might have been impossible for him if I had been a boy—bound as he was by the ghost of the tyrannical patriarch who disappeared each morning into his tea room, returning in the evening with a reason for beating one of his sons. I believe that my father—whatever loss and emotional damage he suffered in this regard—truly hated his father, felt no wrenching ambivalence. I believe that the brutal and regular beating of a child will have this horrifying and diminishing effect as will no other form of punishment.

"My girl," he used to call me when he was proud. And I think he may have meant as well: My girlness.

Yet, there was something. And I now think, watching my older son grow into more and more obvious suggestions of manhood, watching his torso slim and his hands broaden until they near the size of my own, seeing the unmistakable energy of sex in his nine-year-old eyes, hearing him describe his erotic nighttime fantasies with a deeply attractive modesty but with an equal measure of relief at the discovery that they are universal and not his own odd inheritance; I now think, finding myself filled with jealousy—undeniable jealousy—when his most focused interest is aroused by his friends and their world and no longer by me, finding myself holding on to my five-year-old as I never did his older brother, holding on to the time when I am his primary focus, a part of me wishing it would never end—that time when I can stroke his body and bathe with him and draw his passion onto myself with an attentive smile; finding myself, in short, becoming more and more a mother over the years, I begin to think my father's fear of me was profoundly sexual. He could not have accepted the inevitable pull of incestuous desire. He could not have felt anything but horror at these unexpected feelings that his love for "his girls" came more and more to include. He wanted me to follow him into the labyrinths, my willfulness hopefully chiseled into a responsible courage, armed with convictions in the face of inevitable adversity, but he wanted me to follow him fully dressed, and more: well-groomed in a *dignified* manner, a manner which could be trusted to contain the disturbing sexuality with its blood, its discharges, its sensuous odors, its complicated and unpredictable *desire*, that ebbed and flowed underneath.

How could he have known then that this desire, this sexuality, which was the very mark of my exclusion from the heroic quest, would itself become the first labyrinth; that as a woman I would have to follow it through many dangerous caverns, however dangerous, in order to discard the false geographies which were intended only to repress the female spirit and in that sense to deceive.

How could he have known that love itself would have to come into question? My father had instructed me to love men as equals, to expect to be loved that way in return. And yet somehow, he had also left me vulnerable to the foulest of corruptions: the urge to submit for submission's sake; the willingness to suffer humiliation for the sexual pleasure of another; the degradation of that very aspect of my being that he had taught me to respect the most: the assertion of my will. He might not have accepted the inescapable connections for women of my generation between their courage in pursuing the Gift for the People on the one hand; the vindication of the self and the celebration of the female body on the other.

He would have thought the hero was androgynous —and s/he will someday be. But if he had lived a while longer, I would have tried to make him see that, for this generation—in search of a prize which is at once personal and universal—the hero is a woman.

3
The Lessons
of History

The sin so awefully revealed . . .

—Nathaniel Hawthorne,
The Scarlet Letter

1

It was in 1955, the winter of my twelfth year, in the children's section of the Loews Sheridan, that I first felt a boy's hand on my thigh. It came under my skirt as I, trying to appear unperturbed, continued popping buttered popcorn into my mouth. The hand belonged to Robert Wong, whom I did not particularly like although we were going steady. I didn't break up with him mainly because he was Chinese and I had been taught never to insult members of other races. I did not stop his hand from continuing its travels up my leg because it felt so good. The hand tickled the outside for a while, then moved toward the inner region while I cooperatively opened my thighs a fraction of an inch. When I looked over at my best friend, Sheila, and her boyfriend, Bobby Nunzio, it was clear that they were not similarly occupied. His arms were around her waist, hands respectably visible; her arms were around his neck, romantically appropriate. They kissed long, possibly with their tongues, but that, I saw with some disappointment, was definitely all.

Except in fantasy, it was always hard for me to be the first girl to achieve distinction. My determination unhappily often a bit less than heroic, I preferred to follow more brazen friends, daring new adventures only after the path had been cleared a bit. Nevertheless, as I felt Robert Wong's fingers begin to inch their way under my underpants, resigned to the fact that whatever modesty or reticence I possessed had been thoroughly vanquished, I put my popcorn down under my seat and spread my legs.

But move your attention, if you will, as I had to, from the inside of my thigh to the inside of my head. While my body ached for that integration of being that comes with fulfilling the ecstasies of the flesh, my mind whirled with cultural and moral commandments. With military efficiency they lined up in opposition to natural desire so that, far from unified of body and mind, I was becoming more and more fragmented, possessed by the presence of two irrevocably conflicting yearnings at one time: How I wanted Robert's fingers to continue their explorations. And yet how I wanted, how I continue to want, that detached invulnerability which is so revered, which is often the hidden basis of perceived excellence and of beauty as well; that invulnerability which makes it so much easier to be good because it is translated into a true, or at least an habitual, lack of need.

Detachment, antithesis of my real self, would continue to elude me, and I would grasp it only for moments of exquisite peacefulness, and then at a much older age than twelve. That afternoon at Loews, more characteristi-

cally, Unity and Alienation struggled violently for possession of my soul, Unity in the lead for a moment as my
thighs moistened with the sticky liquid called forth by
Robert Wong's precociously adept fingers; but Alienation
finally victorious as Sheila and Bobby unentwined themselves to my left while on the screen, Elizabeth Taylor as
the Jewess Rebecca and Robert Taylor as Ivanhoe remained in unquestioned possession of their dignity, a searing reminder of my own lack of self-control.

By the time I was fifteen, like most of the girls I
knew, I'd learned to present if not thoroughly cogent then
at least passionate arguments in resisting those boys
known to be nothing more than seekers of the flesh. But
our self-deception was as profound as that of the boys. We
both thought they loved our bodies, managing only a
cursory and insidious interest in our minds. The truth was
they loved neither. They were frightened of us whose
desire, once aroused, was reportedly so uncontrollable.
And we, whose deepest sexuality must certainly inhabit
the same region shared by other equally revealing desires
—the desire for power, for example—we were frightened
of ourselves.

At twelve, I merely clutched the purple velveteen
arms of my seat and waited for the familiar fleshy drum-
beat which would release me from the power of Robert
Wong. That accomplished, I adjusted my yellow-flowered
underpants, slammed my thighs shut for the duration of
Ivanhoe, and, avoiding Robert's hand, which, seeking my
own, now searched for proof of more comradely affection, I wept silent tears of mortification and penance
which must have been equal in their bitterness to those of
Hester Prynne, whose archetypal and heroic story I would
one day teach to high-school juniors, emphasizing the

theme of woman's search for self-knowledge through suffering. I suppose Robert Wong thought I was weeping for
the dark and sultry Rebecca who was losing Ivanhoe to
fair-haired Joan Fontaine; but the tears were not nearly
so mundane. They were a rushing, divisive river symbolizing the tearing of spirit from body, of self from equally
precious self.

Robert Wong, I admit with some nostalgia, was only
the first in a long line of admirers in junior high school
whose claims to my benevolent regard were finally disappointed by my passionate and final choice, toward the end
of seventh grade, of blond and blue-eyed Christopher
Clay, a boy who was considered neither manly nor brilliant by the others but who nevertheless was exquisitely
desirable to me, partially, I think now, because he was not
popular and I was.

Popularity, the few times I have enjoyed its pleasures, has unquestionably included that very quality of
detachment it has been my more common fate to adore
from afar. Voted the most popular girl in the class for the
seventh-grade yearbook, I was unpossessable. Desiring attention and affection as much as any other twelve-year-
old, I didn't have to risk revealing myself in pursuit of
either. They wanted me, the boys and the girls, because
my picture owned that highly coveted spot in the yearbook
where I was safely and protectively defined: Most Popular. Unburdened for a short time by the ambiguities of the
heroic quest, I had become instead the prize; while upon
Christopher I projected that other side of my nature. He
would be the one called upon to prove his worth, the one
to need me. Only later, when I was protected by our intimacy, did I secretly hope to find the opportunity and the
courage to reveal my needs to him.

But I came to love Christopher Clay. He had a habit
of squinting at the world as if it were laid out before him
and he, an explorer from a far-off galaxy, had just come
upon it. Like the other boys, he always rode his black
Schwinn into the park in the afternoons, screeching to a
stop near the playground where the girls gathered, halting
there for a moment to survey the scene. He'd come around
the north side and stop. Then he'd squint at us all in that
characteristic way of his, grin seductively, and dismount. I
thought he was utterly masculine: strong, devilish, and
proud. I longed to be his mounted bike, his thighs flung
snug and warm around me.

Which, after a short time, they were—every Friday
evening that I could convince my father to take my sister
to the movies and leave us alone. He often complied, since
Christopher Clay was the son of friends and fellow Communists and, therefore, his respectful attitude toward
women (the seeds of which must surely have been planted
during elementary lectures on the Woman Question) was
assumed. In fact, during one evening when we found ourselves alone, Christopher spent the entire time showing
me his architecture scrapbook, holder of the cut-out and
pasted images of his one fervent dream. In return, I read
him sections of my diary. But it was precisely in that moment of the sharing of dreams that I began to want to
share my body with him as well. I remember thinking as
we pored over the revolutionary structures of Frank
Lloyd Wright: I don't want to wait. I want us to know
each other's bodies now. Christopher was, after all, as the
child of Communists, one of the clan, the kin group, prac-
tically a brother. But more: Christopher loved me. He
was clearly as ashamed as I was of our desires, and that (I
saw the truth of this odd circumlocution as clearly as I

saw the progression of numbers from one to ten) that sacred shame was, like Dimmesdale's, the undeniable sign of his deep respect.

"First he touched my breast," I would tell the other girls the following morning, "then he tried to put his hands in my pants and touch my youknowwhat."

We described every movement of their hands to each other, relieving the guilt as we shared each other's crimes. Of course we never went all the way.

"Did you go all the way?" we whispered on sleepover dates as we snuggled in bed, holding onto each other's realities.

"No," we said, "no, but almost."

The first time we went below the waist was in my living room, the two of us nestled in my father's largest chair, Christopher's wonderful thighs wrapped around my still discreetly clothed buttocks. And I watched his face with a sisterly tenderness I would not feel for another male face for years to come. We held every muscle of our bodies taut and still and we stared in awe at each other's eyes: only his fingers moved. Finally we came, him behind his closed and now soaking pants, me onto my father's orange tweed chair. And then I whispered, "This is wrong."

"We should stop," he said.

But we continued, saving only going all the way for that day far in the future when we would be husband and wife. Which, despite the proletarian splendor of our commitment to the revolution, we desired with all our little bourgeois hearts.

There was someone else I loved while I loved Christopher Clay. Joey was older than I was; I even thought of him as an older brother at times since he was my older cousin's boyfriend. He was different from Christopher— more known somehow. Not mysterious. There was some deep part of him which revealed itself to me easily, effortlessly. And when I was with him I felt myself to be as nakedly obvious to his eye. There was something we knew about each other, something that was not available to clarification through words, and his friendship would remain in my memory undisturbed: an image of a male counterpart. One day that image would emerge again, suffusing men who seemed compatriots with all the softness and intensity of my passion. But in the early sixties, the years of my climaxing adolescence, I could do nothing but love Joey from afar.

His dark eyes gaze at the wall. There are people around. This is a social occasion. But Joey cannot feel comfortable at the party, for he defines himself as a stranger even among those to whom he is closest; he admits little connection, insisting instead that he be recognized as an outsider, which is what he most fears himself to be. Different. His difference in fact lies in his unusual sensitivity, but because he has developed no way of expressing it, his sensitivity chokes him, confuses him with its unconventionality, frightens him and finally makes him habitually morose because of the continuing anxiety which is included in his silence.

He feels himself, not to mention his life, to be absurd, and this is the late fifties, a time in history when much literature and philosophy is encouraging a conviction of meaninglessness in life. The intense political passions which will relieve such emptiness in men for a while and which next will reassess and reinterpret that emptiness in women are not yet fully brought to consciousness.

But even then, his self-definition as *outsider* will for some reason continue to be the most comfortable posture for him, allowing his vision to float unanchored and comfortably uncommitted over the vistas of an unmanageable universe. He seeks the invulnerability of objectivity, fleeing, always fleeing the dangers of confronting the entangled threads of his principles and his needs.

And yet it is his vulnerability to which I am deeply attracted, his lack of protective shell, his easily crumbled walls, his sadness. It is that same sadness which will continue to attract me, that ghost of vulnerability in a man— mirror of my own need—which ten years later will re-emerge as the danger it has again and again turned out to be.

Why is that sense of connection so dangerous? Because it is always ephemeral. Why is it always ephemeral? I don't know, but after a while it always goes away.

Joey sits on a green couch listening to other people discuss serious issues. He wishes he could feel the seriousness as they do, and, in his despair in finding the world consistently ridiculous instead of serious, he mocks and hurts his friends. It is of course himself whom he finds ridiculous. There is some important way in which he has betrayed himself.

Should he have been a woman? Should he have been an artist? What is the missed purpose, the betrayed creation, the throat-constricting compassion that so makes me wish to hold him?

I am fourteen. My older cousin is sixteen. Joey is her boyfriend, and the two of them, Christopher, and myself are in a small shack on the grounds of a country house my family is renting for the summer. We have come here in the late evening in order to make out while the grownups

are drinking and talking politics. There are two beds in
the shack, nothing more. My older cousin and Joey are
entwined on one, Christopher and I on the other. Everyone is breathing hard, making those guttural sounds that
erupt from the throat with intense sexual arousal. Bodies
are moving roughly and energetically across the thin mat-
tresses. But I am finding it difficult to concentrate on
Christopher's passion. I am listening to the other couple.
Maybe they are really going all the way. Would that
sound different? If I listen carefully enough will I be able
to sense the moment when that infamous border, that
mythical line, is crossed? Will I hear a new sort of sigh?
One I have never heard before?

I listen to Joey's sighs, hear the intimate moans of his
passion, mark the moment of his ejaculation (still madden-
ingly uncertain whether it has taken place within my
cousin or outside of her) and I think I am merely experiencing the titillation of the voyeur. Their intensity
quelled, I return my attention to my own cot and to Christopher until I finally come. But I do not experience the
overwhelming orgasmic passion of the true voyeur, because it is not listening to them nor even watching them
that I really want. I want Joey for myself. I feel instead
the angry yearning of jealousy. But I bury that jealousy
almost as soon as it is consciously felt. I am too young to
accept it, to feel the weight of my love and desire for this
boy who is too nearly my brother for any comfortable sort
of passion. He is my cousin's boyfriend. Not mine.

I wonder why the presence of other lovers in the
room, which initially promised excitement, functioned instead to deflect my attention and compromise my orgasm.
When the four of us emerge into the moonlight, I avoid
Joey's eyes.

He is always thinking about the universe, using its incomprehensibility to excuse his own cowardice—his fear of risk. At that point his parents are pressuring him to go to medical school, but he is temperamentally unsuited to this profession. He registers anyway for a pre-med program, and when I ask him why he doesn't stop to figure out something he would like to do, he shrugs his shoulders, smiles cynically, and tells me that people are dying in Vietnam. His own choices thus slackening into the enervated comfort of insignificance, he drags himself occasionally to his classes as he meditates despairingly on and on and on about the absurdity of death.

Or he is thinking about his block, East 104th Street when it was Italian, and the rubble, the drinking, the drugs, the threatening Puerto Ricans from around the corner, the lines of boys and men sitting on milk cartons playing pinochle into the night. He cannot help thinking about these things. As a teenager, when my cousin begs him to study or to come downtown and keep her company, he will often find himself instead on a milk carton, playing pinochle.

He flunks many of his courses, but he flunks philosophy with a flourish and a poignant shrug of his shoulders. He flunks because when the professor conducts classes on the idea of material reality, encouraging debate as to whether ideas are "real" and if they are not, then how do we possess them—and when another student responds that it is a question which cannot be answered because it suffers from inelegant logic and a faulty analysis of inappropriate categories, Joey jumps out of his seat and begins to laugh rudely, insanely, yelling, "People are dying in Vietnam! What are we doing here?"

He undramatically low-passes in English because he gives up reading at seventeen.

Lured by the tranquilizing serenity of the pinochle games each night, he drops pre-med also.

Primarily he is a sensual, not an intellectual, person. When he sketches, which he often does, you can see he has an excellent eye for line, an instinctive ability to translate onto paper the elusive sense of depth in a shadow.

His academic failures, of course, did not indicate lack of ability. He tutored me single-handedly in chemistry, stuffing formulas into my tight-closed brain like one of those bionic heroes moving boulders. I passed with a 65. I would graduate. I would get science credit. I would never have to take Bio. II and dissect a mouse, the thought of which filled me with such anxiety that upon entering the biology lab once with Joey—like the person who commits suicide because she is so terrified of death she is more driven to be rid of her fear than to avoid its object—I decapitated a mouse accidentally by plunging the top of the aluminum cage down hard on his neck when he was peeking out.

While the finiteness and predictability of science appealed to Joey, those qualities repelled me. I read *Two Cultures* by C. P. Snow over and over in an attempt to unify my sensibilities and was never able to retain a single word. I was as if I feared that in the comprehension of the physical universe something would be taken away from me.

I experienced a suggestion of the reason for my antipathy to science when I was pregnant for the first time. I was desperate then to discover the workings of my body and understand the chemical and physical processes upon which my emotional life was suddenly contingent. But as a result of this sustained interest in physiology, I could think of nothing but death. The workings of my body seemed far from miraculous, certainly not trustworthy; rather, it seemed as if suddenly—a wheel gone rusty, an insufficient quantity of some chemical—everything might just stop, and I began to see all my choices, as Joey's had been, drained of the importance I had grown used to ascribing to them, drifting around my head uncentered, their solidity liquefying and dripping away before the judgment of insignificance.

But Joey loved science. He found a comforting, undeniable reality, I think, in physical processes, seeking in human physiology and in chemistry a security which can never be found in the world of ideas, nor in the world of emotions. Science was for him, in part, a way of seeking boundaries, finite explanations in a world perceived as slightly insane, boundaries to a self which tended to be unbounded, capable of sudden, profoundly disturbing revelations. He was the type of child whose sexuality was irrepressible, renegade, habitually disturbing, because threatening, to adults. When stoned on dope he tended to laugh hysterically.

A more recent scene comes to mind. Joey, who is still my friend, is at the center, but now he is in his middle thirties and he and his wife, my cousin, have recently had a child. After ten years of unsuccessful attempts, during which time he has treated us to countless descriptive lectures on the disastrous effects of scheduled sexual intercourse on the potential for erotic arousal in the human male, after many years of that mixture of envy and fear of parenthood which can result in a near immobilizing ambivalence, they have a baby. One day, I watch Joey clean the baby's shit. She is over three months old, so by now he is an expert, and her shit is the heavy, smelly kind which comes after the inclusion of solids in an infant's diet. As he deftly holds her fat little thighs in the air and washes her soft behind with a clean, white, terrycloth rag, I hear him singing to himself, articulating the words of his song carefully, precisely, as if the words themselves were objectively precious:

Ah, Sweet Mystery of Life, at last I've found you.

And I believe he is quite sincere in a way. In the tone of his voice there is laughter, uncynical laughter, as well as deep relief.

2

Popularity, with its coveted sense of detached invulnerability, as well as Christopher Clay himself, did not turn out to be the permanent crutches I'd have wished them to be at the time. I broke up with Christopher, wishing, I told him, to dare the adventurous horizons of high school on my own. But the eclipse of popularity was less a matter of conscious choice. It was simply not, apparently, the royal identity I had assumed it to be, an identity in which one rested arrogant and secure indefinitely like the Elizabethan Tudors, who enjoyed majesty for several hundred years at a time. It was more like being Queen for a Day.

In high school, popularity suddenly fell away from me, and, from a confident and aloof princess, I turned into one of those quiet girls, hovering on the edge of the crowd, stuttering oddly inappropriate remarks, sitting in the back of the class writing English compositions furiously. My clothes were the same, so I knew it couldn't be that. I hadn't gained any weight. But that magical something, that pull that could not be missed when you had it, had undoubtedly been lost. I talked less and less, certain that the others despised me. And almost as bad, I knew that they despised my drawings.

I was attending a school in which students majored in either music or art. In a place which devoted itself to people who wanted to be artists, I had expected support, recognition, to feel, at long last, known. Here, I thought, people would above all understand the need for encouragement and protection. Instead I found the usual New York City school atmosphere—an occasional sensitive teacher lost in a crowd of embittered and impatient bureaucrats; a student body that was being taught to view the making of art as the designing of products which then would be judged by some mysteriously preexisting, holy criteria and placed in a hierarchy of ostensible excellence which was really only a hierarchy of power and taste.

An art major, I spent many hours in the Metropolitan Museum studying the development of realism. From Giotto's stunning accomplishments in the achievement of perspective, I progressed with transfixed attention through the centuries until I finally came to the madonnas of Raphael. I spent Saturday afternoons sitting on the marble benches, surrounded by the near musical silence of the enormous rooms, staring at those Mediterranean women. Their dark faces seemed so real, so utterly unethereal compared to the stylized, pale, golden-hued Byzantine madonnas. These, ruddy-cheeked and full-bosomed, looked instead as if they had just come in from the fields. Their babies seemed more devilish and overfed than precociously wise and divinely ascetic. Perhaps it is partially true, as I am so often told, that my love for Raphael's madonnas was an expression of my longing for reunion with my own dark-complexioned mother, but as I sat on the marble bench, my notebook opened for the description I was supposed to write for class, I was imagining that I saw in those faces the revelation of the artist himself.

How could he have painted those eyes unless he had known them intimately? Instead of concentrating on the distribution of color and line as I was supposed to be doing, I was fantasizing about who the woman might have been. Was she the illicit lover of the artist and the infant Jesus their illegitimate child? Or was the child the artist himself, drawn from some imagined memory, and the madonna his long-dead but, in his mind, still beautiful mother?

I began to question my pursuit of detachment, to see it as a cowardly goal. Not detachment, but autonomy—in the sense of being self-governing—(if not for an entire lifetime, for that would be too much to ask, then at least for the moment in which the work of art was created) was certainly the state of being which had made possible the eloquence of those paintings.

And if the ability to create art was related to the other passions, was there also a link between one's desire for sex and one's desire for a certain kind of power—the power to communicate with others and to be permitted in exchange knowledge of them?

Where were the links between autonomy and intimacy, between sexuality and power, the balance between selection and revelation? At fifteen I could only wish that my art-history teacher would explain in some thrilling lecture the relationship between the personal life of the artist and the work of art.

But, in Music and Art that year it was fashionable to paint subtly colored cubes and triangles expertly shaded in various hues of gray. In sculpture class, I sat next to a beautiful girl who created a clay plaque of carefully measured ovals and squares. She was the perfect manifestation of the respectable, ethereal woman who always seemed to come in blond. As she worked, she flung her flaxen head this way and that, its clearly tinted silver streaks flashing before my entranced eyes like ocean sunlight. I could hardly keep my mind on my clay for watching her graceful movements.

In the meantime, I fashioned a portrait of my sculpture teacher, a rugged, gnarled, downright Gothic masculine face. And the more I envied my classmate's soft, smooth, peach-colored face powder and her shining silver-blond hair, the more gnarled my sculptured face became. No wonder my teacher didn't like it, criticized it for being too realistic. It was undisciplined, he said; it missed the opportunity for the containment of intensity which can be achieved through a more poetic, abstract form. Was not this containment, he asked me as he poked the wire tool into the indiscreet lumps of cheekbone and the mountainous forehead of my piece, was not this search for the *discipline* of the emotions, the achievement ultimately of pure and balanced form, the very essence of fine art itself?

I had no idea. I was terrified to answer. Betraying my love for the indiscreet madonnas and the fiery Van Goghs and inwardly acquiescing to his judgment of the minor degree of my talent, I decided to switch the next term to pottery (a course which fell several rungs lower

on the ladder of aesthetic seriousness) in order to fulfill
the requirement of a year's work in clay.

In short, I was more and more alone. When suddenly and without warning the prince of the junior class
fell in love with me. He was president of the student gov-
ernment, captain of the basketball team, and first violinist
in the orchestra. He had extremely small, white hands
which I detested immediately, but suddenly everyone
began to treat me with a certain deference, an undeniable
respect. This was too seductive a prize to be lightly refused, so, despite Gerald Burman's hands, I petted with
him on the second date. In this way I hoped to hold his
interest. Furthermore, when caressing my crotch, neither
the smallness nor the whiteness of his hands was particularly apparent, and, having conveniently forgotten my lessons in Loews, I allowed him to do as he wished.

But Gerald Burman did not appreciate my passion.
Instead he condemned me for participating in the embrace which, ten minutes before, he claimed to desire so
desperately. Finished with our petting, he'd emit a great
self-pitying sigh which meant: Why has it been my mis-
fortune to fall in love with a whore? Then he would lecture me on morality, exhorting me to stop him the next
time if I wished to earn his respect. Once he informed me
that if any boy did to his sister what he had just done to
me, he would kill him.

Wild with increasing confusion, I asked him why he
kept doing it if he thought it so wrong. But seeing the
shock in his eyes at this obvious manifestation of my intellectual density and moral degeneration, I quickly reversed
myself and pretended to see, after all, the logic of his
position.

It wasn't that I cared for Gerald Burman. I was

afraid of his power at school. I thought that in order to keep him I had to seem the slave of my indecorous desires, which I would, if given the choice, banish forever. But whenever we were alone and he began to touch me, I proved myself to be without much self-control. All of this was complicated by the presence of another boy in my life whom I liked much more than I did Gerald Burman, but who only seemed to like me when he couldn't have me because I was known as the girlfriend of someone else. I was incapable of resolving these overlapping contradictions in my life, and I approached my weekend dates with both boys with great trepidation.

I was right to be afraid. One Monday morning, following a Saturday-night date with the boy I liked, during which we had petted long, damp, and wonderful hours on his living-room rug, which in turn followed a Friday-night date with Gerald Burman during which we had petted less ecstatically but just as long on the roof of my building, I found the following poem taped to the entrance of my official class:

> To have her you don't need a car,
> On the floor she will let you go far.
> What she likes the best, is a hand on her breast,
> And to kiss with her mouth quite ajar.

Under which was a small picture of a girl lying invitingly on the floor with my name written across the left breast pocket.

The publicized stigma achieved its purpose: already guilt-ridden, I now felt utterly exposed. But I was uncertain of the precise nature of my sin. Was it desire itself? But surely girls in these progressive times were supposed to have desires. Or was it that desire, which Gerald had warned me ought to have remained hidden, had been so inelegantly revealed? Then what in that revelation had been so unacceptable?

My stomach heaved. I breathed short, desperate breaths. My cheeks and eyes burned. I had thought to control my life wisely and I had dismally failed. I rushed home in despair and mortification, closed the door to my room, turned off all the lights, and lay down on my precious, black-spreaded bed to mourn. I was mourning my life, planning methods of suicide, imagining the reactions of all my relatives and friends, telling myself I'd be exonerated by my suffering.

When suddenly I knew that I was completely and utterly alone. If I had been thoroughly misunderstood by Gerald Burman and whoever else would choose to believe his characterization of me as a nymphomaniacal, soulless and morally insensitive slut, then at least in the face of the extremity of their lies I could not avoid the opposing assertion of what I knew to be my true self. It was an early experience of self-consciousness achieved through that internal act of rebellion. I came upon a hint of who I was because I knew that I was not what Gerald Burman thought me to be. My *sense* of my own subjective being: a girl tossed and turned by extreme emotion and unsuppressed yearnings, was enriched for the first time by an objective voice: a voice born of thought as well as feeling, a voice which claimed Reality, objective, external Reality as its rightful possession, a voice which would begin to allow me not only to feel in response to the actions of others, but eventually to initiate personal, social, even moral action myself.

That afternoon, evening, and dark night which I

spent crying on the bed, however, I was conscious only of an unexpectedly comforting sense of aloneness mixed with an unidentified sense of loss.

Having flirted for the last time, during adolescence, with Popularity, the mantle of the unsullied princess forever out of reach, I stopped, if only for a time then still firmly, outside the gates of convention. Terrified and greatly exaggerating the degree to which I had become a pariah to my schoolmates, I became an observer of the social scene rather than a passionate participant.

Years later, meeting old high-school friends as adults, I would discover the full extent to which my utter alienation had been fantasy—very few of them would remember the incident. But the fantasy served to allow me to experience solitude for the first time in my life. I had to learn to sit in class alone. I had to learn to eat alone. And if I was far from contented in my aloneness, if I could not even begin to achieve a sense of separateness which can be a trustworthy protection for extreme vulnerability, I could at least avoid continual exposure in retreat.

I vowed to hide.

In college I would be grateful, at least for a while, for this increasingly comfortable position on the outskirts. Eating in the cafeteria, confidently alone, I would notice other lone eaters leafing through the magazines in which they were obviously uninterested, looking down, learning the difficult lesson I had mastered in high school—that often, when you feel yourself to be the most conspicuous, no one is noticing you at all. I walked serenely down the forsythia-lined path to Cohen Library, where I spent many hours roaming through the stacks. And free of the anxious burden of relationship I began to feel at home within the tradition-scarred walls of the English and social-science buildings of CCNY. I enjoyed that aloof but broadened inner vision that belongs to the outsider.

In my first semester, huddled in my dark-green loden coat that I only took off at home, I fell in love, from a rather safe distance, with the young assistant professor who taught calculus for liberal-arts majors. He was a Polish man who looked and spoke like the engineer on *Star Trek* and who advised me, as a treatment for depression, to read Nietzsche, after which, he promised, I would dance. He often walked me to the subway since his class was the last one of the day, and sometimes he accompanied me all the way downtown. But he must have decided at some point that I was too young and naïve to bother with, as I certainly was, and as a sad consequence our love affair was never consummated. To this day I think of him and how sweet his embrace might have been. He sincerely believed that equations illustrating the limits of numbers as they approached zero were beautiful. Finishing a long problem, he would stand away from the board and regard his efforts.

"Beautiful," he would say. How could I not believe him? I was at that stage of life when I believed that anything declared to be the truth by a good-looking professor certainly must be so.

(Once I had gone to the office of my sociology professor, another handsome man in his thirties, to discuss the relationship between personal psychological pathology and culture-wide neurosis. He asked me—begging my indulgence if it seemed his question was somewhat unconnected to the train of my thoughts, the links would eventually become clear to me, he promised—what my feelings were about oral-genital sex. I had tried this par-

ticular activity just once in my seventeen years, with a boy
named Murray Tannenbaum, who insisted it was the only
way to prove I really liked him. Ever since, I had a recur-
ring dream that my mouth was filled with bubble gum,
and each time I tried to pull out some of the gooey, pink
blob, it would grow bigger and bigger inside threatening
to choke me to death. I enjoyed Murray's penis pushing
into my throat in neither cultural nor psychological terms.
When he came, I hid my face in the quilt, hoping to muffle
the sound of my gags. Still, I engaged in a long discussion
with my sociology teacher and dutifully attempted to seek
the elusive connections between this exchange and my
original question. If the connection remained obscure, it
must surely be because of my faulty intellect. Probably I
would only get a C from him.)

For my calculus teacher I went home each night and
pored over my math book with an intensity I had previ-
ously reserved only for romantic poetry. It was not the
problem but Mr. Petrichkin's face that drove me on,
and the only time I ever saw him distracted from total
attention to his mathematics lecture was when a girl
named Rebecca with a large, round ass, tightly covered
with a straight black skirt, jumped up and ran out of the
room for a drink of water. In those straight skirts, running
was no small achievement. You took little, fast steps and
necessarily wiggled your ass from side to side as you pro-
ceeded. Mr. Petrichkin stopped dead in the middle of his
lecture and watched her leave the room. Then he sighed
audibly, sighed with deep desire and stoic resignation. It is
the sound of that sigh that stays with me to this day whenever I think of the embrace I missed.

While sorry for the loss of the more carnal aspects of
Mr. Petrichkin's love, I was nevertheless comfortable with

my newly won reticence, believing that virginity of the flesh—like purity of the mind—was not something relinquished in a moment forever, but rather a state of being one could recapture if, for a long enough time, one did not indulge. Recalling the self-righteous feeling enjoyed when, due to rigid dieting the pounds begin to drop away, I gloried in the thought that with a stoic and meager sexual diet, reduced to an occasional weekly allowance of masturbation, sin would drop away as well. And my favorite poem, the one I typed out, framed, and hung on the wall above my bed, was the verse from Swinburne:

> From too much love of living,
> From hope and fear set free,
> I thank with brief thanksgiving
> Whatever gods may be,
> That no life lives forever,
> That dead men rise up never,
> That even the weariest river,
> Runs somewhere safe to sea.

The relief I sought, of course, was not death but the conscious suppression of emotion. The weary river was not the river of my life but of my feeling, and the sea was the place where I was nurturing a kind of containment for the seedling of my separate self.

I developed a deep attraction for nuns. I would stare at them unashamedly as they flowed down the street in their long, black coverings. I would imagine, discarding inconvenient knowledge of shaven or cropped heads, lush auburn or silken blond tresses carefully braided (their wildness controlled) and twisted into a precarious bun beneath the veil. Many were truly beautiful, and it was shocking to discover that womanly sensuality would prevail even when only the face, from hairless forehead to chin, was visible. Some were young, their untweezed eyebrows and skin free of cosmetics attesting to the existence of a sort of beauty we were unwilling at the time to risk; there were also those whose old and tranquil faces suggested wisdom to me, a wisdom born of their withdrawal from the world of love and a commitment to the spiritual life.

But more than anything else I saw them as being invincible, out of reach. And when I turned my attention to the boys in my various classes, I was inevitably attracted to those who also seemed to possess such qualities; whose own aloofness would serve as a continual reminder of my psychic goals; whose stern self-discipline could be counted on to punish any unwary infraction on my part in the direction of unleashed hysteria—however close that hysteria might bring me to grasping certain truths. I looked, in other words, for my opposite, someone who would not only represent an alternative to my true character, but who would judge me as well.

I was sitting in the cafeteria drinking coffee when I met him for the first time. He sat down at my table and began to talk about eighteenth-century poetry. The neatness of Pope's couplets thrilled him. He was inspired by the order of his style. He blushed with passion as he extolled the discipline of the poet's emotions. I was attracted to his passion, and to the fact that he loved what could be counted on to deny it or at least keep it under control.

Unlike the "intimate" poetry of John Donne, I would read in the introduction to the collection he showed me, "Pope was always conscious of the actual rather than the imagined audience." (The imagined audience was the lover of the poet or the poet himself, whereas Pope's poetry was always directed to the Public.) The characteristic fiction of Pope's poetry, I read, "is not that of a man undergoing experience but that of a man who has already undergone experience and is now conveying what is representative in it, what is socially viable, to his peers." And bringing what had been only vague suspicion into clear consciousness, the editor continued, "Donne and Pope therefore are dramatizations of different *stages* [my italics] in the intellective process. . . . Pope unlike Donne is reticent about revealing his inner self."

I talked all afternoon with Colin O'Connor about these contradictions, and despite what I ought to have seen in Colin's cold, blue eyes, and what I ought to have heard in his passionless description of his poet laureate's distrust of extremes of any sort: a clear warning of misery to come, I dropped English 42A, *The Romantic Poets*, and registered instead for English 42B, *Dryden, Swift, and Pope*, where, heart throbbing with an intensity which might have been a suggestive reminder of the life I had sworn to be done with, I found a seat next to Colin and began, in only several days' time, to start wearing high-heeled shoes and lipstick to school.

My only weapon in this new immersion was the recently developed and still precarious vision of my treasured objective eye. Sensing its importance only by instinct (what I sensed, I think, was that there was a space inside me where I remained constant, untouchable), I clung to my sense of it, never revealing its existence, counting on it to come to my aid when I needed it—as it was becoming increasingly clear I very soon would.

Colin's best friend, the closest intimate of his soul,

was Vinny, a fellow Catholic whose praises I heard sung every day, whose Friday-night date with Colin was sacred and could never be supplanted by a need or desire of mine, and whom I never met. Sometimes, however, before he met Vinny, Colin would walk me home from school, a trip which, since it covered a distance of seven miles and was periodically interrupted by browsing in bookstores along the way, took close to three hours. I relished this allotment of time with Colin when we would argue the relative merits of Keats and Pope, when he would tell me, to my delight, that I was both the only girl who liked to look in bookstores as much as he did and the only girl he ever fucked who enjoyed it; his former sexual experience being limited, it must be admitted, to a girl named Theresa who, in Colin's bitter terms, resented the intrusion he represented into her thoroughly douched and perfumed vaginal canal.

When we came home from a Saturday-night date—I often wondered if the mysterious Vinny hated my claim to Saturday as much as I did his indisputable possession of Friday—we would wait for my family to fall asleep. My father always slept with his good ear to the pillow, his deaf one turned to the world, so there was no threat of our being discovered. And then I would change into a yellow, tentlike dress with nothing underneath. After great amounts of foreplay, which I somehow always had enough self-respect to demand, I would sit on Colin's unzipped lap so that while he entered me, my great, wide dress covered us both. Just in case my father ever awakened, he would observe nothing more shocking than lap-sitting, that is if we could manage to turn our desperately ecstatic expressions into ones more appropriate to the sort of Platonic friendship my father always hoped I would pursue.

But Plato, I would one day discover in a transforming essay by an anthropologist named Stanley Diamond, was the very man who was originally responsible for the intellectual tradition which reveres abstractions of all kinds—the tyrannical definitiveness of one, finite idea, one Form, which reduces any diversity to diversion, any passion to pathology, any conflict to civil crime. And that very tradition was the one waiting in the wings to devour me in the form of Colin's belief in Virtue, in Sin, and in the persistently attractive Purity, however frigid, of Theresa.

One weekend, when my family was off to the country somewhere and I had the house to myself, I invited Colin to sleep over. How full of promise and warmth the solitude seemed, how fraught with varied possibility its four empty rooms. "Just imagine," I sang to Colin, "how wonderful it will be to fall asleep together afterward, not to have to hide under my yellow tent dress, to use our eyes as well as our hands . . ."

But that was the last thought Colin could tolerate. What he loved to touch in the darkness, became too unsubtle a manifestation of his guilt in the light, and, instead of making love when he came over Saturday night, he began to talk about Theresa. Why couldn't I wear high-heeled shoes to school every day like she did, he asked meanly. (I had reduced my days of elegance to Mondays, settling for more comfortable loafers, upon whose heels I did not continually stumble, for the rest of the week.) What did I think of dying my hair blond, he wanted to know next. And then, in a final cruel wounding, he in-

formed me that Vinny, the adorable, witty Vinny, had
over the months come to refer to me as "Colin's Saturday-
night Jewish whore."

Colin showed no interest in my theory of Vinny's
jealousy, nor any receptivity to my analysis of his and
Vinny's friendship as unusually and even strangely (I ac-
centuated the word *strangely* aiming in retaliation for a
weak spot) devoted. No, he said. The point was that his
relationship with me had forced him to rethink his reli-
gious convictions. Clearly, he finished in a logical tone, he
was still more attached to Mary and Jesus and the moral
implications of their virtue as taught by Saint Paul than he
had thought.

"But you told me," I begged, "that you were finished
with them and that Theresa represented all that you hated
in the repression of sensuality." He looked down at the
floor with a genuine helplessness.

"Pope and Swift didn't deny the joys of the body,
you know," I continued. "Passion might be resisted but it
wouldn't be repressed." And I quickly quoted a passage
from Pope's "Eloisa to Abelard" I had memorized:

> In these deep solitudes and aweful cells,
> Where heavenly-pensive contemplation dwells,
> And ever-musing melancholy reigns;
> What means this tumult in a vestal's veins?
> Why rove my thoughts beyond this last retreat?
> Why feels my heart its long-forgotten heat?
> Yet, yet I love! . . .

"Your favorite poet," I argued, "doesn't revere
frigidity born of the inability to feel—you're a passionate

person, Colin," I said, knowing I was wrong. "You can't escape that."

I could see, however, that I was losing Colin when he abandoned his clever language and deft insults and began to tell me of his true suffering, his indescribable sense of guilt for our lovemaking. He told me of a tormenting memory from childhood. At the age of twelve, he had gone to confession with a friend, a former Vinny I presume, and having already experienced many breaches of faith, frightened that Mary Mother of God was perhaps not as incarnate as she was believed to be, having actually considered suicide as an alternative to the loss of faith that was threatening him more and more unavoidably, he sat as near as possible to the confessional in order to overhear the deepest sins of his friend, hoping to discover that he was not alone.

He heard the other boy describe a sexual encounter with a neighborhood girl in painfully honest detail, evoking the feel of her small breasts, the irresistible taste of her tongue in his mouth. But the priest interrupted the boy's attempt at spiritual honesty by yelling at an indiscreet volume and, according to Colin, with the unmistakable desperation of the true voyeur ringing in his voice: "YES, BUT DID YOU GO ALL THE WAY?"

Colin O'Connor, laughing hysterically, ran out of the church and vowed never to return except when absolutely necessary in order to prevent disclosure of his now certain heresy to his devout mother. Describing the incident to me as we sat holding hands on my bed, he began to cry.

"The loss," he kept saying, "you cannot comprehend the loss." And as I held him against me, I knew we were lost. I loved him though, so I began to assure him that we were better off as friends. Didn't we love to browse through bookstores together, and take seven-mile walks through the city? Surely we might continue these activities even if he decided to reclaim his purity and try to forge a way back into the arms of the church—which he clearly could not do without. He was quick to accept my compromise solution, so quick that even at the relatively unsophisticated age of eighteen, I knew myself abandoned. And I was certain as he walked out the door, leaving me in my now barren apartment, whose every room threatened loneliness instead of promising riches, that there would be no bookstores and no walks, but only retreat again, a reunion with my at least already identified inner eye.

"The ecstasy of the Romantics," reads the editorial introduction to Colin's collection of the poetry of Pope, "is best described by the line of Browning's: 'the pain/of finite hearts that yearn.' But soaring, like creeping, is for the Augustan poet a mode of motion inappropriate to man, whose place is firmly fixed, and upright, on the earth."

"What we cannot overcome," said Pope, "we must undergo." And that sentiment, at least, was as descriptive of Colin's involvement with savior and saints as it was of my more temporal pain when, predictably, I began to see him around the campus with Theresa on his arm, her blond hair perfectly coiffed, her high-heeled shoes clicking rhythmically. She would never creep as I had done, sucking Colin off though I still hated this form of lovemaking (it should perhaps not be tried before the age of thirty) only because he loved it so. But she would never soar

either, I told myself vindictively. There is fear and loath-
ing beneath the apparent civility of those whose separateness and autonomy have never been tested. There is a
difference between true autonomy, which includes a
capacity for intimacy, and a frightened distancing, which
increases until the space around you becomes layered with
veils which cannot even be lifted at will.

Like Giotto trying to shrink someone down to size
when viewing him from afar, I try to shrink the memory
of Colin. But he remains enormous—not because my love
for him is unextinguished. I have long ago given him up to
the victorious Vinny, the lovely and reportedly pure
Theresa, and I do not even know what has become of
him. But still, the power associated with his memory will
not diminish. What stays with me to this day, painful and
haunting, is the memory of him wanting me, but always
under the yellow tent dress.

4
The Marriage
of Opposites

You fill me with guilt, eternal boy, you too aren't loved the way you'd wish to be, you'd have done better with a wife who peeled your apple, mended your clothes, worried about your silver and your china, shared your love of land and little tribe, your fear of people and of loneliness. But I with my searches, my nightmares, my causes, my need for crowds and solitude, what a burden I must be. Who are you? Can we really ever know each other? Is it dangerous to ask?

—Francine du Plessix Gray,
Lovers and Tyrants

1

At the end of *The Scarlet Letter*, the cowardly Dimmesdale is dead. The vengeful Roger Chillingworth is wasted by his bitterness. Pearl, the love child, is liberated from continuous expiation and from narrow-minded convention by the unusual events of her early life and she becomes both mother and adventuress. With all the principles of the drama dead or gone away, it is Hester, one-time pariah, who returns "of her own free will" to the scene of her infamy, where her stigma now becomes the

mark of her superiority, of her considerable knowledge of
the human condition, of her unique creativity.

The women come to her for advice:

> . . . in the continually recurring trials of wounded,
> wasted, wronged, misplaced, or erring or sinful passion
> . . . [they] came to Hester's cottage, demanding why
> they were so wretched, and what the remedy! Hester
> comforted and counselled. . . . She assured them too of
> her firm belief that, at some brighter period, when the
> world should have grown ripe for it, in Heaven's own
> time, a new truth would be revealed in order to establish
> the whole relation between man and woman on a surer
> ground of mutual happiness. Earlier in life Hester had
> vainly imagined that she herself might be the destined
> prophetess . . .

Hester has reclaimed her sexual passion into herself.
The same self which had been revealed to Dimmesdale in
love is now, at the end of her life, revealed to the towns-
people through a personal and charismatic autonomy
which permits her both unusually sound moral judgment
and sympathetic psychological insight. Her creativity and
her sexuality have come from the same source. "The sin
so awfully revealed" in the opening chapters of the book
was not merely the sin of sexual desire, but the assertion
of the female self. Dimmesdale was not the only man who
would neither understand nor welcome that self-governing power. As for women, we would often resist the as-
sumption of such responsibility with equal intensity ourselves.

Hester's psychic journey from the privately asserted
sexual self to the publicly acclaimed wisewoman—a

woman whose knowledge of the self is rooted in experience—is the journey from the Shameless Hussy to Shaman. The Shaman is the archetypal mother, an older
woman who possesses a spiritual power derived from an
awareness of her own vulnerability and thus an increased
capacity to tolerate pain, and a political power which
emerges from personal experience and allows her to guide
her children through the inevitable dangers and challenges
of the heroic path.

But who was the Shameless Hussy? She was the girl
with no restraint, willful and without pride; the girl who
lay on the bed, whose stockings always tore; the girl who
lost control to the touch of a boy's hand softly in her
vagina making it ring and ring and ring in satisfaction; the
girl who insisted on writing poems that were considered
irrelevant to the universal concerns of humanity, and if
not exactly irrelevant then certainly undignified and
aesthetically unappealing—poems about menstrual blood;
poems about female sexuality; poems about motherhood.
She was the girl whose father called her a Shameless
Hussy.

"He called me a shameless hussy," a young woman
said to me in a women's group, her blond hair glistening,
her small breasts hardening, her taut cheeks flushing a
lovely and desirable rose. I laughed at the phrase when I
heard it, thinking it picturesque, thinking, mine only
called me whore. But it took time to understand the full
meaning of the phrase: not only that desire was unquench-
able and unextinguishable and far from understandable,
but that we said so. Openly. And at length.

Whom did the Shameless Hussy love? She may have
seemed indiscriminate, but beneath the apparently hap-
hazard pattern there was a deadly accuracy to her choice.

I buried her again and again, differently at different points in my life. After I had children, I buried her slowly, not with a rebellious bitterness but with an anxious and ambivalent relinquishing—a slow tearing away of a dearly loved part of myself. I thought that if I contained her intensity in the world of work and banished her from love, she would grow to be less of a troublemaker, would finally succumb to my control. And that may still turn out to be the truth.

My daily life for more than five years was primarily involved with work and children.

I pondered continually, even obsessively, about women and their art. How do we transform the facts of our lives into words and images which are at once balanced replicas of the knowledge we have torn from the heart of our experience and at the same time slight distortions, but distortions which ironically reveal more of the truth than would a precise mirror?

I thought for months at a time about the distinctions between fiction and autobiographical nonfiction. I have read beautiful novels about love which are clearly the personal confessions of the writer. I have read open confessions which are well-constructed novels. But unlike the critics, the word *confession* conjures up in me thoughts of heroism, the promise of a moment of comprehension of the universe through the revelation of the self. There are poorly written ones, to be sure; but some of the greatest works in the history of mankind and womankind have been confessions: the tearing off of the writer's skin in an attempt to get down to the beating heart: an action rooted in a faith in our immutable kinship, in the belief that in the experience of one human being can be found the character, or at least the history, of the race. Rousseau's *Con-*

fessions. The Interpretation of Dreams. Fear and Trembling. The autobiographical fiction of Colette. Tillie Olsen's "I Stand Here Ironing" and "Tell Me A Riddle." The poetry of Adrienne Rich. Doris Lessing's *Children of Violence.*

In the service of building an emotional history of women, I tell myself, I, too, must tear off the skin, expose the lies publicly.

What I have discovered has to do with love. The personal knowledge I have gleaned leads me, just when I least suspect it, into history, into politics. But there my father sits and waits for me, and I grow frightened. When I remarked that for a woman today sexuality was the first labyrinth, that if my father were alive today I would insist to him that in entering that labyrinth my search would be every bit as political as he believed his to be, I underestimated, like any hero beginning on her naïve and hopeful way, the enormity of the resistance I would discover in myself: the resistance to continuing. The urge to turn back tempts me even at this moment. I wish to stop this writing, to put this book away and go on to another, perhaps to put writing itself away.

I get a job teaching. Gingerly I open the cave doors for twenty-five students. They peer in and determine how long to look. There is no fear. We are twenty-six people together. No one will be allowed to get lost. No one for that matter will be allowed to go too deeply into the caves; not here; not now.

We talk of our mothers as shamans, inspired by Maxine Hong Kingston. We step into caverns where tools of the witchcraft our mothers used on us are displayed for the daughters to view respectfully. We turn to the few men who share the class with us and talk clearly and without subterfuge of the false and ludicrous expectations we have been taught to have of each other. Adrienne Rich reminds us of the long-buried erotic depths we all feel for women. During a panel discussion on loving other women, a young heterosexual woman, beautiful and intelligent, speaks of a close friend whom she has been afraid to love sexually.

"I am afraid of having sex with her," she haltingly admits.

"Have no fear," says a young gay woman joyously, somewhat lasciviously, sympathetically, assertively. We all laugh—and for those of us whose sex has been directed to men, a question moves about the room, establishing itself before each pair of eyes just as surely as if a math teacher were holding up one of those cardboard math cards for a group of third graders: $9 + 9 = ?$ Our card says: Would sexuality expressed with other women free us of the immobilizing complexities it involves with men?

But we don't risk answering here. Instead we look at each other kindly. We gaze into each other's eyes. I allow these young women to feel me as a mother: a woman with children, a guide who identifies the dangerous and provocative sights. Next to each display of our psychic history we note the torn bodies of the women who pointed the way: Emily Dickinson. Simone de Beauvoir. Tillie Olsen. Doris Lessing. Adrienne Rich. Toni Morrison. Ingrid Bengis. Lynda Schor. Maxine Hong Kingston. We gaze at each other again. Silences have their impact. Some take notes—a means of establishing a veil between the mind and the image before it. Some are noticeably uncomfortable. It is early in the term. We have not yet reached the section in which we will deal with love between men and women: fathers; brothers; lovers; friends;

sons. I am preparing them for that harsh part of the journey. It will be harsh because their guide has come to wonder what hope there is for us in this generation. At the same time she has recently experienced love for men in ways she thought she had safely buried. She has felt deep pain. She has felt the Shameless Hussy rising into visibility, tangibility again. And with that precious touching of the old self she is nurtured and cannot merely feel regret.

I refer to myself of course. I slipped into "she" because I spoke of myself as a teacher, the point being that teaching young people the complicated psychic and political history of the last ten years is more exhilarating than dangerous, and its relative lack of danger comes from the fact that it is one step away from an authentic confrontation with the self. If one teaches, one must guide. And this assumed identity serves as a kind of protection against vulnerability. After class, we may all go out for coffee, our vision now softened by what Virginia Woolf called "the cotton wool of every-day life"; by mutual humor; by the joy of understanding each other; by hot coffee on cold mornings after a very early class.

I wish to teach these ideas, but not to write of them. Writing is magical. There will be no distance, no protection, and I am afraid.

I am a woman trying to understand love. I am trying to understand how the uprooting exhilaration of the first months of expressed passion can become, in a short period of time, the source of pain, of loss of self.

I have come to believe that the exploration of woman's sexuality, her ways of loving, is an enriching road to the understanding of complicated issues of autonomy and creativity. Feminism has returned our bodies to us. There is a connection here I wish to explore, a connection I have always felt in myself. If I can bring sexuality, as I have felt it, assertively into the open, then I will achieve one more step along the way of the discovery of the self.

I am interested in exploring the mysterious process by which marriage to an exotic lover is transformed by the roles of parenthood and a life of devotion to children into a love more kin to the love of siblings than any other, moving between a quiet, even a contented domesticity and a rage nurtured in the deepest regions of the heart, the place where all love once thought new merges with its ever repeated origins in incestuous desire. I want to know why in the early morning I wake to see the dark blue light and cry in pain that the depths of passion and intimacy I once hoped would be mine are not mine but only flood my early-morning fantasy which by that evening will be transformed into a mature and moderate fatigue.

And yet, when I find the very passion I had thought to seek and want so desperately, I feel myself cut from my moorings, wandering unclaimed, and I am brought back to that tiresome and obsessive search for who, after all, I am.

I am reminded of the joke about the man who decided to retreat into a cave to contemplate who he was. After ten years he discovered he was a hermit. In order to discover who I am as a woman I have children. After eight years I discover I am a mother. In order to discover who I am as a woman I begin to write every day for years, to discover finally that I am a writer. In order to discover who I am as a woman I fall in love. I reread Simone de Beauvoir's words on "The Woman in Love" written twenty years ago and discover that I am the woman in love.

Once again I learn that the word *love* has come to have no specific meaning. Even death and excruciating long absence do not dull the feeling of connection to those I love. But I am interested in the specificities of language. I would strike the word *husband*, for example, from the language. Its original meaning: "one who controls and administers with prudence and authority" is clearly insulting, and ever since I discovered the precise meaning I have winced each time I use it as a means of introduction or convenient identification. I would substitute various words which would be descriptive of various stages of the relationship. A lover may become a brother or an enemy. In either case, his relation to me is enriched or diminished by the degree to which he is a mother or a father. After all, in some sense everyone I love is either my father, my mother, or my sister. Including my first child. My second son is the only person with whom I am on deeply intimate terms who appears to retain a psychic integrity within my incestuous and devouring mind. I do not have any idea why this miracle occurred.

My *husband*, then, after a few years of being my lover, became my mother. But when our first child was born, for his own familial reasons, he turned much of his attentive intimacy toward his son. He, after all, had his own incestuous agenda, his own myth to live. But in that moment of changed direction, however slight, of his affection for me, he slipped from mother to father, and finally, since he did not become an enemy, into brother. Our passion turned into a wonderfully predictable security within which I, at least, flourished for quite a number of years.

There was a man in my life wanting me sexually as often as I wanted him, who came home every evening, called when he would be late, slept beside me each night, instructed his colleagues to wait if he was talking to me on the phone during business hours; who, in short, because

he was by now my brother (devoted and identified), assumed all of the responsibilities of love that men generally resist so strenuously. I was a very lucky woman,
people said. But to label this complicated process of our
relationship: *love*—would only end any further analysis
or even communication. Don't think: she loves him. Certainly don't think: she is in love with him—an even more
confusing phrase. Think more specific even if more
lengthy thoughts: She feels a deep sisterly devotion. She
depends on him. She has come to need his quiet, consistent strength and his self-containment just as surely as she
has come to hate the negative side of these qualities in his
nature: his infuriating distance; his emotional passivity;
his walls. She feels affection; dislike; but above all connection. It is this increasingly inexorable link, this utterly
familial sense of belonging that I wish to understand.

I want to understand, because as much as I value the
link a time came when it didn't seem nearly enough—
when to feel it as sufficient for my life would seem as
strange as reducing my love for women and my intimate
friendships with them to my feeling for a biological sister.

I am a woman of periodically strong sexual drives,
and I say this with great ambivalence. I am ambivalent
because strong sexual drives, whether or not they are expressed, deflect energy from more lasting satisfactions.
Perhaps if I were not burned with a consciousness which,
however changed by the history and experiences of the
last eight years, was nevertheless formed originally in the
forties and brought into moral articulation in the heavily
strictured and deeply contradictory fifties, I could casually
and without emotional debt simply enjoy my sometimes
intense sexuality.

I became a devoted and conscious feminist between

the ages of twenty and thirty-five. I work and have great
need of my work. I have at least three enriching friendships with women in which we do not fear being either
mother or daughter to each other. I am a mother. After
eight years I can finally pass by a mirror, look in, and say
with relative conviction: I am a mother. For many years I
had very little contact with men. They hovered on the
edge of my daily life, appearing mostly as husbands of my
friends, an occasional editor, a professor, an analyst. The
ghost of my father stalked the house periodically, issuing
familiar commandments with respect to dignity, warning
against excess and revelation, sneering at my habitual
dungarees. But I consoled myself that ghosts who had
been virtually vanquished deserved a free run once in a
while—just for reminders. And anyway his warnings always pertained to boys/men, whereas my life, or its energy, was—except significantly for my family—devoted
to women.

Protected, then, by the illusions which come so easily
when I retreat into a tunnel vision, I came to think I had
grown out of an old way of loving. I thought I had left
certain habits behind. I had thought the "narcissistic
woman in love" as described by Simone de Beauvoir in
The Second Sex and read about avidly by me at the age of
twenty-two was a safely buried part of myself, as effi-
ciently transcended as was Colin O'Connor himself, or my
guilt for preferring the passion of Keats to the elegance of
Pope.

But I found that the old questions returned. For how
many generations is love to be poisonous to a woman's
autonomy? Ought her sexuality, because of the psychological vulnerability it carries within it, to be denied, eventu-

ally even repressed? Can she relinquish the deep pleasure of a penis within her much as she would relinquish chocolate cake for life if she were allergic? And can she perform this amputation upon herself without a price? Can she develop the ability, learn the method, of touching her most profound erotic sensuality in response to the body of a woman? And is sexuality, if expressed with other women, free of the dangers which seem so inexorable an aspect of its expression with men? Or is it sexuality itself, with its physical merging and orgasmic loss of self-consciousness, which threatens to return me too completely to an infantile need for an adoring mother, a panic in the face of the separation of the self? Is even frigidity a tolerable price to pay? Can one be relieved, as de Beauvoir suggests in a recent interview, to discover love literally frozen if its heat has in the past given only the pain of interminable, anxiety-ridden ambivalence?

I undoubtedly spoke too haughtily of the veils of others that could not be lifted at will. Veils of my own still remained to be discovered that would prove so unsusceptible to being lifted at will that upon discovering their existence I would be shocked. They had grown so close to my face over the years I hadn't even known they were there.

Perhaps there was a simple, biological reason for this new intellectual obsession. In my thirty-third year I was possessed by a renewed and reawakened sexuality. My friend Helen, commiserating one day over a glass of wine, assured me that as of the week following her thirtieth birthday, her own thighs were almost constantly wet in the presence of a wide variety of men, and we happily decided that, like our small children, we were going through a normal, developmental stage. I would stop my work several times a day to masturbate. My pants, in the presence of certain men, would moisten from vaginal juices whose aroma, I felt certain, could inform at least a square city block of my embarrassing state.

Soon after I became aware of this discomforting fact, I began to seek out friendships with men I knew with an interest I had not felt for many years. What they said about their lives seemed relevant to mine. During that period of time, Adrienne Rich published a new poem entitled "Natural Resources," in which she first describes the old and precious hope of women that somewhere there exists "the lost brother/the twin," "the phantom of the man who would understand," "the being with natural resources equal to our own"; and then she dismisses this hope as phantom indeed, as certain illusion. But the image of the lost brother filled my imagination once again: perhaps after these long years of warfare with the male sex, I would find him, that once certain phantom, to exist after all.

But by now you understand the kind of question by which I am obsessed. And if it is clear that my motivation for the intellectual quest is to seek some understanding of the emotional needs and conflicts which, without conceptualization, can cause a horrifying mental paralysis, I cannot apologize for this direction of the analytic process. I believe that all intellectual quests have emotional and sexual links, but to certain people these links become more apparent than to others.

I am a feminist who has feared and hated men and who all the while has continued to love them. That love has reemerged now. I have torn off the veil of self-control and transcendence and found myself to be as vulnerable as ever. So I need to discover the meaning of this *love*, throw the label away and find what is festering underneath.

I need to know what I must sacrifice if I treasure my autonomy. I need to know what I can never sacrifice if I value my wholeness.

2

A young woman and man in their early twenties walk arm in arm down Fifth Avenue. They have a strong affection for each other, having recently separated from a tormenting two-year marriage. Their sexual and emotional obligations to each other thus relieved, since they were clearly unmatched in both respects from the start, they are free to feel a renewed sense of mutual connection: links of respect, attraction, intellectual companionship that initially held them together in college feel secure again, and for several months after their separation they share the comforting illusion that they will love each other always. The woman is me. I feel comfortable with Brian's arm around me in this way. I have thought of him as a lost brother, pushing to the edges of my consciousness his working-class Irish background complete with heavy drinking, unpredictable violence, and a horrifying Calvinism that includes the classic identification of a woman's body with the devil and his seductive work. But I am no longer dependent upon this man for sexual fulfillment. I am growing thin again, whereas while married to him my thighs and stomach had thickened upon the excessive diet of his dislike. I am free once again to enjoy his poetry, his true sensuality and romantic humor, since once again I can enjoy them for themselves, hoping for no promise of their genital expression between the sheets. We walk, joke, talk about literature in the way that people in their twenties do when they are seeking to impress themselves and in that impression of the self create an aspect of what may in fact become an authentic identity. I am dressed attractively, in case along the way I meet another interesting man with whom I might wish to have a love affair. It is 1966. I see my women friends—mainly the same two women with whom I still share my life—only when we are "free" for the evening—that is, when there is no prior commitment to a man. I am man-hunting. I want the sex that this brother-husband denied me for two years. I want to feel desired. I want to desire in return.

A man sits on a stone bench and rises to greet me as I pass by, my shoulders leaning into the arm of my former husband. He is clearly very glad to see me, and, in that moment of his rising when our eyes meet, I remember him and remember that I had been wanting to meet up with him now that I am unmarried. He is black, and I have never had a relationship with a black man, but I am not worried about this complication prematurely. I have always admired both his eyes and his hands, the first dark and sensual, the second long and graceful, suggesting all the intimations of control and competency which my own hands lack. I have seen him move glasses of Coke and cups of coffee across a crowded lunch table when we worked in the same office, and I thought that those hands, unlike mine, would never spill the Cokes all over the laps of the diners. I was not surprised, therefore, when I learned that he had been a waiter carrying large, silver trays of dishes and glasses in Atlantic City restaurants, that he had been a short-order cook manipulating huge wire vats of sizzling french fries. I shook his hand, grasped it firmly, introduced the man I was with as my ex-husband, and went home to wait for his call.

He begins to call me quite regularly. I do not have to sit by the phone and wait for his call because he always calls before I can grow impatient. Since I am practicing liberty, I tell him frankly that I hate the woman's role of waiting by the phone so I would like either to feel free to call him or to make our dates before we leave each other from the previous date. These instructions on my part prove to be unnecessary, because in a very short time he brings me home from a date and never leaves again. He keeps his own apartment for several months just for safety's sake, but he moves his TV and his hi-fi into mine, and so I am relatively secure of his intentions. I think I have no desire to marry again, having recently divorced. I am contented with his company.

I do not feel the uprooting passion for this man that has gotten me into so much trouble in the past. I feel a quieter love growing for him. I am stunned again and again by his consideration and his kindness. I grow to like him.

My best friend complains to him of the problems of her marriage. Her husband will make love to her only once every month or two, and he tells her this is natural for people who have been married for over two years. I watch James as he advises my friend. He is honest and supportive. Eventually, it is he who will help her move her furniture into her new apartment when she decides to leave her husband. I watch him carefully. With a great reasonableness I click off positives and negatives on a mental balance sheet.

Despite the racial difference between us, everyone in

my world, including my father, is impressed with him. He is strong. He is stable. He will—so the theory develops—contain me. I have finally found a man who will contain my "wildness"—who will create a haven within which I can develop some self-control. When we have our first child, my father will express far greater confidence in James's ability to hold the baby and quiet his cries than in mine, even though I am the mother, even though I am nursing.

Although I have always been the strongest person in my family, using my mouth and my will to win for my father, my sister, and myself whatever I think is our due, although I have proven myself, if nothing else, a worthy defender of my father's wishes, when he dies and we discover his last letter to be opened upon his death it will give clear instructions for his somewhat unorthodox funeral, and it will end with the paragraph: "I know that my sisters and some of my friends will want to go against my wishes for my funeral arrangements. I leave it to my *son-in-law* to see to it that my wishes are carried out."

I will never forgive my father this slight, this disrespect, this final insult.

And yet, were I looking for a person to trust with my last wishes I would choose James, too. Were I looking for someone to lean on . . .

The thing is that he is in every way the opposite of the difficult, ambivalent Jewish male like my father. Compared to this emotional difference between us, the racial issue is minimal. Perhaps his emotional character is culture-wide, or has an important cultural aspect; perhaps I, like many an anthropologist, have thought myself to be intimate with an individual—gaining knowledge which would be appropriate to a personal journal, a record of one woman's experience, only to discover that what I have learned belongs instead in a chapter on culture and personality.

But for me the cultural difference, when it assumes any importance at all, is not that he is black, but that he is not Jewish.

There is no mirror here of myself, just a deeply refreshing foreignness. Like that anthropologist visiting an entirely new culture, I am learning rules and expectations I have never come across before, witnessing strengths of character I had thought to be only mythical. For example, James almost always says what he means, never giving the silent instruction which utterly contradicts what is being said. When my father said, *No, of course I don't mind,* he might very easily have meant, *Yes, I mind very much.* One had to understand the real message from the context, the facial expression, from past history. But James says he doesn't mind only when he doesn't mind. He will not, therefore, develop elaborate punishments for not heeding the silent instructions. This quality has given me, the astonished anthropologist, years of pleasure.

However, the aspect of his difference which turns out to be the most important is that he never seems to have the urge to articulate his feelings. He is the ultimately taciturn man. He has the feelings, has them deeply, and is intuitively sensitive to the feelings of others. But he never wants to talk about them and, if asked, he does so resistantly, eventually angrily, after having been pressured to do so by me for more than ten years. I will never understand this habitual silence, since for me reality assumes clarity only when it is described, and described, and described. One or two descriptions will never suffice to ensure its permanent existence. *But you see . . .* I will say to my husband over the years, when he has already seen hours before. *On the other hand*, I will continue, exploring every nuance of every feeling I had regarding a certain experience with the wild and hungry expression of a lion after its prey, with an excitement that now James will view with the eyes of the astonished anthropologist and ultimately with the exhaustion of the anthropologist who has remained in an exotic culture one year too long.

This inclination to remain silent about his internal world will stick with him no matter how hard he tries to temper it for my sake. It is an intrinsic, deeply ingrained part of his character. For years I will try to change him. Next I will struggle to accept his difference from me. But I will come to believe in the permanence of this difference only after eight or nine years of struggle. During the period immediately following his father's death, an incident occurs which forces me to acknowledge its permanence because I will finally understand its depth.

James's mother, right after the loss, calls and visits us very often. I become very involved with the process of her mourning and so, only by necessity then, does my husband, her son. One night when we are in bed she calls us in an hysterical state. She sobs for a long time on the phone repeating *It's so bad, it's so bad.* Then she tells me the story of the heat coming up in the radiator.

The sound of the heat was something she had always loved. The weather would be turning cold: Crisp air, a stream of it, coming through the slight opening at the bottom of the window; the beige nylon curtains moving in and out, billowing, in the way she loved to watch, not ever understanding what it was about the movement that so delighted her but looking forward to it in the early mornings as if she were reuniting with some long-lost loved one instead of simply watching nylon flow in and out, blown up toward her, then pasted for a moment against the window with the autumn wind.

The early morning had been her favorite time of day. When her children were small, long before it was time to fix five breakfasts and begin the day, she would rise, dress, and sit by the back door with her coffee. Just to feel the morning. It was a moment of peace, a place to rest before the start of the day.

Even in New York, when there was no longer a back door or the sweet smell of the season, she would walk to the window, her husband, William, asleep in the bed, and stare out at the city. She was alone. She thought about things.

With the increased cold of the October days, the heat would be turned on in the building and she would hear it knocking and banging through the radiator as it forced its way through the pipes, warming the room. Now that the children had gone into their own lives, she would sometimes get back into bed and push against her husband's back, reaching around his body to hold him, while she listened to the radiator rattling. Something forcing its way into the room to gently and slowly replace the cold. The heat coming in. The window opened so that the cold morning air could tease her cheeks with a pleasurable discomfort. The curtains billowing. His back moving slightly in and out with his sleeping breath. Her morning coffee finished. Her solitude of the morning complete.

Now the heat is coming through with no one in bed to move against, with William colder than October wind deep in southern ground, and the rattling and the banging of the heat is driving her mad. She closes the window, sobbing. She is forever extinguishing small pleasures: she does not dare to get up early anymore to have her coffee, that solitude now a tormenting symbol. She will get up with just enough time to dress quickly and leave the house; she will eventually run out of coffee for months, settling for instant at work. Mornings are over for her. She wishes only to sleep longer and miss them. But the rattling in the radiator is the worst of all because it cannot be extinguished. With the heat turned on or off, the radiator still knocks. And the sound is enough to bring the rest of it back to her. Cold air. Curtains. Coffee. Solitude. Rattling heat. She sobs and screams, scared that the nice young man from next door will think a robber has broken in and that she is being attacked. But she can't stop. She will go mad. Or maybe this was it, this was going mad. Uncontrollable screaming. Huddled on the floor tearing the lime-green nylon of her gown. The sound of the radiator, the sound of loud drums announcing William at the window, William at the door, William leaning over her, and then gone: his side of the bed empty.

Presently after the whole story is out, she wants to hang up. Having given me the details of her pain, she is filled with an almost pleasant tiredness. She wants to go to sleep.

I hang up and turn to James, telling him, "Your mother's hysterical." And I relate to him the story of the radiator, after which we both lie there silently.

I am thinking: what if it happened to me? What if James died? And I slip immediately into fantasy, trying to find the single point through which I can thoroughly understand my mother-in-law's experience.

It would be the feeling of the quilt, the warm quilt, I think, that I could no longer bear.

If one of my sons becomes a novelist one day, he

might begin a book with this paragraph: *My mother was always cold. When we left the house each morning it was never before she could wrap an extra muffler around our necks, pull a sudden woolen cap down over our ears, cram some last-minute gloves into our pockets. On rainy days in the spring we always had to wear boots. The other kids wore sneakers in a spring rain.*

The feel of the quilt at night, even on a warm night, is exquisite to me, but its feel has been linked with the feeling, to my right, of James's thigh. I feel the quilt lying gently on me and become suddenly perfectly conscious of James's thigh resting next to mine. Quilt on top. Well-known and well-loved body to the right. That double feeling bequeaths to me an enveloping peace. Being warm. If I wake at night, if my children are asleep and I don't have to get out of bed, I am often thankful to be awake so I can experience this feeling: those two simultaneous touches against my flesh which are somehow the same touch; like the feeling children get when they play the game of crossing two fingers and running a pencil between them. What is really one pencil feels, because the fingers are crossed, exactly like two. But if you open your eyes, you will see every time that it is one pencil.

Crying by now, due to the reality of my fantasy as well as the full comprehension of my mother-in-law's pain, I turn to James, then intrude upon his perpetual silence and ask, "What are you thinking?" hoping for once to be answered from some vulnerable depth, some imperfectly achieved separation.

And he admitted (it was an admission because he was incredulous himself at the fact): "I was thinking about the Knicks. Wondering if they were going to trade Frazier."

He shares this disconcerting ability to separate himself from the most intense events of his life with his mother. It is a quality I have often admired, certainly envied. It is an emotional strength I have tried to emulate in order to mute somewhat my excessive involvement with others, my unconscious slipping so easily and so imperceptibly into fantasies of merging. It is the quality of character in James which has caused me to feel as sublime a security and as profound a rejection as I have ever felt in my life. It is a madness which is so entirely different from my own that for many years I mistake it for sanity.

3

Had it not been for my paternally nurtured desire to find work which would be self-defining, had it not been for my tendency to lose my boundaries in an uncontrollable merging with those I loved, I might have ended up living with a different sort of man.

Yet there must be hidden, secret functions to this marriage of opposites. Otherwise why is it sought so often? Why is it so prevalent? Why does it provide so much security during one stage of life only to become so insufficient during another?

I examine it from the point of view of a woman like myself: that pole of the opposition who may easily lose control, whose emotions and deepest feelings are dangerously close to the surface, mystifyingly accessible in a world where most are busily searching for their feelings, so that she must spend her life struggling for self-control just when others are trying to break down the barriers. While tempted to give in to what will come easy for her, the free expression of feeling, she must search instead—in the words of Ruby V. Redinger, a recent biographer of George Eliot—for "the self that self restrains." Perhaps it is the woman writer or artist of whom I speak. Or simply the human beings, men or women, who as children were the wild ones, the ones who by some inseparable combination of genetic inheritance and family conditioning, were difficult, uncontrollable, dominating. Oh (always the risk), perhaps I speak only for myself.

There is a connection for me between the ability to feel autonomous, to feel confidently creative, and a fear of certain kinds of love. The love, especially when it includes passionate sexuality, undermines my ability to be myself, pulls me away from open channels, reawakens in me a desire to succumb to the ferocious power of my father's needs.

An aspect of that threat is described toward the end of *To the Lighthouse*, when Virginia Woolf reveals the struggles, the vague feelings, the thoughts which accompany a woman artist, Lily Briscoe, in the precise moment of creation. In this scene, the largely unexplored connection is sought between a woman's search for autonomy through work and the dangers to her of released sexuality —of love; between the yearning for reunion with the loved mother and the fear of desperate attraction to the powerful father; between her rejection of the quintessentially maternal woman and her rejection of the childlike, needy, and demanding traditional husband. In the moment of painting her picture, of struggling for the accomplishment of the first few lines, all these themes come together for Lily, but they come together not as a purposeful, abstract examination of the relationship between her own artistic confidence and her sexuality, but rather in the manner of an inner flow of consciousness which moves from vague sense to external action—from a fleeting image of Mrs. Ramsay to one clear brushstroke; from a sense of anxiety in response to Mr. Ramsay's demands for attention to a sudden moment of focus and concentration on the painting.

In the moment that she picks up her brush, dips it into the paint, and brings it to the canvas, in that defiant artistic leap between "the planning airily away from the canvas" and "actually taking her brush and making her first mark," various levels of her consciousness open up and flow into each other. The connectedness of her being is fully illuminated. The first level of her attention is on her craft, her willingness to begin the process of what is often a painful intensity of focus, a kind of backbreaking concentration. Alongside of this primary concentration is that function of mind which the poets have called reverie; to which psychoanalysts attempt to give a method in the process of "free association"; what people who are not analytically or rationally minded often just call thinking or daydreaming. The distinction of the artistic process is that the reverie is in the service of that primary level of focusing on the concrete demands of the work of art. It is in this sense that the artistic process is a metaphor for any exercise of free choice. There is a moment in which, though all of one's contradictory feelings are conscious, though the risks are clear, a human being takes a step that is not necessary according to any abstract value but only according to the demands and requirements of oneself. It is in the moment of any kind of creation—a new way of life or a work of art—that the experience of autonomy is to be found.

Lily, all the while painting, driven by issues of line

and composition, thinks first of her own temperament, of her isolation, of her mysterious drive: "this other thing, this truth, this reality, which suddenly laid hands on her," and which is what separates her, painfully and yet kindly, from much of female humanity, from being an "ordinary woman"—the sort of woman so perfectly epitomized by Mrs. Ramsay. Then Lily thinks of her art—her feelings about her own art and the demands of Art itself, how it insists upon worship, and she wonders why she continues struggling over and over again to be born. Her doubts, her lack of confidence in herself as an artist and particularly as a woman artist, are concretized by Charles Tansley's words, which echo throughout her reverie: "Women can't write; women can't paint." These doubts flood her mind as she paints. In an almost musical duet, two Victorian dancers moving across the floor, she paints a stroke and then she hears: Women can't paint. She paints another line and the words come once again.

But soon, behind her now fully achieved concentration, she is aware that "she is losing consciousness of outer things." There is a feeling of her mind having opened up, of an almost physical sense of open channels linked together where before there were only impenetrable walls of flesh. Many thoughts are rushing internally, thoughts which still seem to be unconnected, and yet it is her painting that is calling them all forth. The reverie is harnessed and the dozen or hundred or thousand associations gallop rhythmically, obediently, behind her eye and her hand, instruments of her concentration.

"Her mind kept throwing up from its depths scenes, and names, and sayings, and memories, and ideas . . . while she modeled it with greens and blues."

Lily recalls whole scenes from her past with Mrs.

Ramsay; she imagines what is happening at that moment as Mr. Ramsay and two of his children make the trip to the lighthouse never made by his now dead wife. She mourns Mrs. Ramsay. She yearns for and then once again rejects for herself Mrs. Ramsay's most essential quality: her overpowering maternal femininity; her acutely developed, eternally practiced nurturing of her flowers, of her guests, of her children, but above all and most perfectly achieved, of her husband. Lily, the artist, the creator, is of course also the "odd woman" doomed simultaneously to self-expression and self-doubt. By a temperament which is strengthened by conscious choice, she cannot give that everlasting caretaking to a man. It is not that she is insensitive to them, not that she misses their cues and signals. She hears Mr. Ramsay ask. But she will not give. For she sees clearly the price she must pay if she assumes this most tiring, this self-sacrificing, this creative female work: the work of loving and giving and sensing—always exquisitely sensing—the nurturance needs of a man or a child.

"That man, she thought, her anger rising in her, never gave; that man took. She, on the other hand, would be forced to give. Mrs. Ramsay had given. Giving, giving, giving, she had died—and had left all this."

Naturally Mr. Ramsay is very agitated at her refusal and he finally elicits a compromise from her: she praises his boots. And even that small gift is enough to restore him, so utterly dependent has he always been on a woman's verification of his worth. It is not difficult to understand Lily's succumbing to temptation, as we have all along understood her ambivalence toward love. When Mr. Ramsay has been fed, he is a fine man to behold. He is at once paternal and sexual. Perhaps he is even brilliant

—or, still more sympathetically, *he might have been brilliant* except for his unusual devotion to his family. He is magnetic. He is precisely *not* the lost brother, the man whom we might look straight in the eye. He is the father-son with whom most of us fall in love most of the time. For at the very same time that he is the embodiment of potential male genius, of powerful male history, he is also a small boy needing his mother to whisper behind him: "Don't worry. Go ahead. You can do it by yourself."

"Why, at this completely inappropriate moment, when he was stooping over her shoe, should she be so tormented with sympathy for him that, as she stooped too, the blood rushed to her face, and, thinking of her callousness . . . she felt her eyes . . . tingle with tears? Thus occupied he seemed to her a figure of infinite pathos. He tied knots. He bought boots."

This father and genius and powerful man was that vulnerable. And yet she had tormented him, had refused him the depths of her attention. She must be an unnatural woman, she thinks. And by the criteria of long-followed sexual custom, indeed she is. Her commitment to her self-expression through her art must be that rigid because it is that precarious; if she succumbs once, relinquishing her sexual attention to him, she may be thrust down Mrs. Ramsay's road. So she continues to paint.

Her reverie goes on for many pages. But it is clear that her concentration is still on her painting, for she prays that no one will disturb her, and she finds it "merciful" that no one does. Though she seems to be in a trance, underneath "all her faculties are moving with extreme speed." She no longer feels the pain of this opening up, this speeding internal movement, only the intensity. She would not stop now, and yet a part of her probably waits impatiently for it to pass. She mourns Mrs. Ramsay again, the mother-person with whom she wanted a deep intimacy which she never achieved. And now she cries out for it: "Mrs. Ramsay!"

But, insatiable, she wants Mr. Ramsay too.

Lily seeks to express what is universal at the core of her being through the particularity of a specific artistic vision. While she struggles for precision of line, the core keeps appearing, visible for a moment and then transformed into something else. First the core seems to be her need to create art in the first place. Then it appears to be her long-felt passionate love for Mrs. Ramsay, her search for union with that supreme mother-woman. It darts about her consciousness once more, shadowed temporarily by her attention to Mr. Ramsay's boots, spotlighting the compelling nature of his need for her, for woman.

In the end she places a decisive line on her canvas and she lays down her brush. Her life has passed before her, held in this one connection: her feeling for Mr. Ramsay as he bent down to tie his boots. And in the context of her refusal of him, she found the strength to finish the picture that perhaps "would be hung in the servants' bedrooms. It would be rolled up and stuffed under a sofa."

Can anyone think it irrelevant that a woman wrote this description of a woman making art? In accepting the sacrifice she must make in the male-defined world of love, Lily Briscoe is able to accept herself as a woman artist—if only long enough to paint her picture. To the Lighthouse is in the mode of confessional literature because it is concerned with the revelation of the self for the self. Since it is always the case for any artist that the work may very well end up under a sofa or reduced to ninety-eight cents on the remainder shelves of used-book stores, since that painful consciousness becomes an aspect of the process of creation, there can be no other purpose to a life devoted to the making of art than self-revelation. It is when self-revelation misses its link with some universal aspect of human experience that its worth diminishes.

The value of confession as a mode of writing, the value of the need for confession as a motivation for writing, lies not only in its provision of clear points of identification for other women, but in its intellectual method. It is not only in order to communicate the ideas which have emerged from my experience that I write, but to transmute the felt authenticity of those ideas by revealing the experience which gave birth to them. And it is always the experience that is primary.

That is the fate of the Shameless Hussy. She is unlikely to fully grasp abstractions which are unrooted in experience and is therefore often in trouble, periodically a troublemaker. It is only when she has stepped back from the new experience, usually both hurt and exhilarated, that she is capable of the sort of self-knowledge that might be the first step of an insight into human history. But first the experience must be shared, the confession made. To deny this sequence in the development and clarification of my thoughts would be to fall into a passionless abstraction and thus to lose the heart of the truth.

So my promised obsession with sexuality has inescapably broadened into a more difficult search for knowledge of the self, which for a woman often demands that she find a way of life in which she acts from motivations of inner conviction and not from a desire to please.

Like Lily Briscoe, I work in order to separate myself from the power of my parents' image of me, and at the same time I use my desire for separation as energy for my work. The two paradoxical struggles are perhaps eternal ones, but for a woman that primary desire for merging through love in childhood is socially encouraged, repeatedly and painfully re-created, in the later world of sexual love.

The strength and impact of Woolf's description of a woman in the act of creation, in the moment of the separation of the autonomous self, lies in the recognition that the smallest details of behavior, the subtlest communication in the external world of love, may nevertheless be sufficient to draw a woman away from her work—from her self-definition. The use of my own name if I am married, the maintaining of my own desk—not sharing a single drawer of it—these are unimportant details only to those whose sense of separateness is thoroughly secure. But I identify with Lily Briscoe, who is precisely not the artist so engrossed by her work that she is untempted by love; instead she is the woman who consciously chooses to limit and even change her way of loving, because to love utterly, offering herself up in the bargain, continues to be so very tempting.

It is because she understands the price that she chooses as she does. Having chosen, she doubts herself again. And then she chooses once more.

The need to work, which I have nurtured so carefully in the past years, is a need which is linked to conscious values of political feminism; but those values are rooted in the knowledge that the work of developing the separate self, the work of separating from early parental nurturance or deprivation, cannot be achieved through love alone. I often write frantically, for with each completed section I rest momentarily alone, secure within my boundaries, my autonomy symbolized by the existence of that now external creation: the work, the piece of writing. Boundaries then release their tautness and temporarily relax into flexibility. The chaotic tendencies of a self that comes easily uncentered are held in the finite work. The frantic, driven aspect of the need to write, as well as the panic during periods of inability to work, is in that sense a panic of non-being. I may lose myself too easily in a reflection.

Is it that I seek to recapture a memory of once experienced union? Or is it that the moment never existed after all? Are we each doomed by having had the experience of union to search for its reexperience forever, or, having had it, are we free to grow? Is my great desire to become one with something or someone beyond myself a compensation for deprivation or a search for a repetition of a once known paradise?

I marry a man who will not allow me to come too close because that seductive merging might return me to a desire for non-being, for lost boundaries. The prohibition, like any strong taboo, derives its potency from the depth of its appeal. It is the appeal of the loss of self I am fighting, the universal desire for periodic loss of self in love is made gigantic and monstrous by the fact that I am everywhere encouraged to lose myself in love: love of children; love of a man. This is the point at which my deepest sexuality merges with cultural history and why the means of changing the direction of the second can never be achieved without confronting the potency of the first. Sometimes I fear I will have to sacrifice sexuality itself in the struggle for autonomy. Many strong women do. Still, the search for wholeness is apparently undiminished. There will be a time when I will seek this unity again, the exquisite moment of unconscious being which can be achieved when the self is reflected in another, the momentary loss of self whose perfect metaphor is sexual passion and orgasm.

The Shameless Hussy would choose a man who promised passion and not restraint. Unconcerned with art or politics, she courts the blurring of boundaries and teases her sense of self with the romantic promise of perfect intimacy. But then she also risks the continually recreated pain of separation, the searing realization that she will always be alone.

Over and over I will have to bury her passion in order to transcend her vulnerability. Each time I bury her it will be with a deeply felt sense of loss. Each time I dare allow her back into my life, I will have to blind my older eyes to her past anguish saying, That? That was not pain. Only lack of knowledge.

But that will be years later. I will find the courage to awaken her only after I have been engaged for years in the drawing of boundaries: through motherhood, through steady work, through a marriage of opposites—only after I have become acquainted with the exercise of my power in aspects of life besides sexual love.

My mind during the first decade of my marriage to James has not muted the memory of danger. I am as relieved as my father to think that the Shameless Hussy is under control at last.

4

There are many times in my life of outward change, fewer times of consistent patterns, when I feel I have grown used to a certain way of feeling, a certain way of behaving, so that resting in the security of a stable self I am contented for a while. But although the times of change are more frequent than the others, it always takes a long time to recognize them. Perhaps it is that they are not one solid period in a life but rather a movement, changes within a greater change, periods of increasing adjustment to a new layer of self. Perhaps it is that while the external world is moving along into new experience so that I can hardly grasp its finitude on a given morning—a child is born; another child enters school; a book is published, a job changed, a friend divorced; a treasured relative is dead—the internal world lumbers along unwillingly, even imperceptibly, sometimes refusing to move at all.

The first stage is my refusal to recognize that another change is upon me. It is my period, I will think. I am overtired. And then I will try that old, trustworthy explanation, satisfying because it obliterates will and responsibility: Well, I will say, I am mad after all. Here it is again—my madness. I cry and am sad for days. I dream so intensely that I awaken in an exhausted state. Frantically, I try to search my dreams for clues, to understand messages. But I cannot. I write them down, page after page in my dream book, waiting for some explanation, for some symbolic key like the convenient key one reads alongside *Finnegans Wake*, providing explanations, interpreting symbols. I write them down. Perhaps next week a pattern will emerge.

One day I become suddenly aware of what is happening. I am talking to a friend and he asks me how I am. I talk about sadness, about my nerves, trying to discover in the audible sounds of my voice the secret I had not been able to unlock in quiet thought. And suddenly it comes to me. I am changing, I say, and know it is the truth.

A part of me frozen for more than eight years cracks the ice of my everyday life and rises up again. I feel my sexuality like an internal ocean washing through me, choking my by now habitually rational tones, pouring through my mouth chaotically, washing down my body, around my thighs. I am always wet, wet with desire, wet with fear, wet with a new and terrifying cleanliness. For years I had loved women, closed my eyes to men in fear of their betrayal, in rage against their cowardice, thinking I had accepted the disappointment that they will never love me in the way I wish to be loved. I had even grown to relish my loneliness, accepting the fact that I felt utterly bereft of male friendship, utterly without the depths of male sensuality I once dreamed of possessing, in that sense utterly alone.

I make love regularly. I close my eyes and give in to my unacceptable core, feeling it become slightly more acceptable over the years than my father would have wished it to be. Often, I come.

And yet there is ice which covers each opening. For years there is ice. Why suddenly, in the middle of my thirty-third year, did the ice crack, upsetting the carefully created balance of my serenity born of a newly won ability to sacrifice? Why did that part of myself long compromised to secrecy begin to emerge again? And what crucial shadow of potential was emerging in the flow of my sex?

Perhaps it was only that I was nearing thirty-five, "a woman's sexual epiphany."

I first heard that women in their thirties are notoriously sexy when I was twenty-two and an English teacher. In my fourth-period English class sat an eighteen-year-old Haitian boy who wanted me. He told me all about the girls he fucked each week, and I desperately pretended to give grown-up understanding while begging him to remember his upcoming English regents, assuring him he was talented and sensitive. Confused by the fact of acknowledged, simple desire, I insisted he was a poet. Once he asked me directly to do it.

"I am engaged," I said.

"So what," he answered sensibly, having been fucking since the time with the kitchen maid when he was six and wealthy, not yet a refugee from Duvalier.

"No, I can't, Etienne," I said. "Because I am your English teacher. We have a regents coming up. Have you read *Hamlet*? Have you finished *Silas Marner*? Do you even know the difference between a subject and a predicate, for God's sake?"

I thought I could motivate him to study if I inspired him to write poetry, to grasp the connection between the depths of his feelings and the expressiveness and control of language, the way one can be used to protect and nourish the other. But he asked me again to have sex with him.

"Can't you ever think of anything else?" I demanded, glad to be the asker of that question for once.

"I'm eighteen," he said, as if that were all the explanation consciousness required, "and when a man is eighteen he is at the peak of his sexuality. A woman reaches hers at thirty."

"Well I'm not yet twenty-three," I said and gave three compositions in a row a red *C*.

Or perhaps it is not my own age that is critical, but the age of my children, the youngest out of babyhood, his eventual independence and ever clarifying separation from me forcing my attention elsewhere—whether from an instinct for self-protection or self-expression I am not sure. But I watch my friends with babies, mark their complete erotic focus on the needs of the child, and I remember how I was that way. In the moment of remembering I understand that I am that way no longer. I feel the change only subtly at first. I sense men again with my whole body. I no longer avoid them at parties. I am afraid of my desire, recalling its ugly, self-destructive, and infantile aspects. But when I feel my back straightening and my cheeks more often flushed, I know the change is irreversible. Enormous change signaled by a small, delicate, physical sign.

Once before I remember change announcing itself in this way. I had been lying on a hammock under an apple tree. I was visiting my friend's family in their country house and, selfishly leaving the responsibility of the young children to the others, I'd sneaked away. The leaves and boughs of the apple tree hid me completely. No intruding eye could have discovered me. I lay back, looked at the blue triangles of sky, little slivers of precious sapphire, and I rested my hands on my thighs. I was reaching back for something. At some point in my past I had been lying in a hammock touching my thighs like this. I closed my eyes. My thighs had been young and strong from two months of summer swimming. Reaching back, I felt them peeling slightly down the front. I had been swinging under an old oak which stood in front of a house where I had spent my childhood summers, a place which returned to my dreams like a faithful friend each time I was subject to chains of repeated nightmares, a place that meant uninterrupted, simple growth.

Under the oak tree (under the apple tree) *I touched my thighs and closed my eyes. In the distance I heard children screaming, children not much younger than I was. They were the little kids, the younger brothers and sisters.* (They were my children.) *I changed position on the hammock, sighing with pleasure. I was free. The grown-ups would attend to the little kids. Occasionally, looking in my direction they would talk about me. Rocking like that, one foot dangling into the wet grass, I relaxed into their definitions of me, their expectations, existing in a comforting passivity, without choice.*

Under the apple tree, I stroked my thighs, slightly flabby from childbirths, and thought bitterly: But now I have to organize life for these children so that they can rock and dream under the apple tree.

Change, I said aloud to myself, relishing for one more moment the feel of the wet grass between the toes of my dangling foot. Then I got up to help with the children.

It is so minute, the internal sign of change. You touch your thigh and in the difference of its feel you know that your life has turned on its axis and your eyes, ripped from habitual and comforting vistas, are looking at something entirely new.

Slowly the parental protection I receive from James

becomes insufficient to my life. I used to love lying through an entire evening near him, saying almost nothing, just feeling his presence—the television would be on, perhaps, the radio . . . lounging and luxuriating in that exceptionally passive love. Now I am restless, dreaming of exotic passion, adventure. I drink a lot. Smoke dope.

One day I will ask James to break down the walls with me, confess to him that I am fearfully weary of being alone. What is in his heart, what memories keep his head so rigid, what longing and cries unanswered keep his gaze in so focused a direction?

Behind the walls I see a small child in a playpen. His mother is not quite eighteen and she already has three children. The two older children are kept in a playpen for most of the day while she attends to the baby, but the two older children are no more than babies themselves. They are naughty—that is the neighbor's interpretation of their continuous cries. They cry and wail each time they need their mother, but frequently she doesn't come. She is washing, nursing the baby, cleaning, fixing the elaborate meals her husband demands. She is pregnant with a fourth child. The boys in the playpen learn that their loud demands will not be answered. They learn to play for many hours by themselves. They learn to stop demanding, to stop crying, to be strong.

I cannot blame James actually for not wanting that wall torn down. He sees the baby learning to take care of himself, learning to be alone and not bother his mother. He sees it all as clearly as I do. We both look at the baby and imagine what he must have felt. We are abstract and analytically descriptive. Why should he be burdened with the actual memory, with the recollection of feeling, with that loudness and the agony of the unanswered cry?

I tried to tell him for years that I didn't feel him with me at the deepest moments of my life. The time came when the protective distance between us seemed more a desert than a moving river, and I tried to cross it, to preserve something, to avoid loss.

He said: I am happy where I am. Stop trying to pull me out.

He said: I'm sorry you often feel distant from me. I want you to live with me here. But I have a way of life that suits me.

Why after all should he seek identification with his mother's pain, struggle to feel the loss of the rattling and knocking in the radiator? With that knowledge of her life, the walls might break down. The little boy in the playpen would lie beside me in my bed. I would hear his cries.

And yet, unsympathetic, devouring, I will ask him to do just that. I will ask him to risk hearing the child cry, because I believe that in the sound of that cry, in the memory of rage and loss, lies James's buried need for me. Not a need built on weakness and fear, a desperation to control, but a fine and proud need residing in the most vulnerable core of the self without which you perhaps can have a friendship filled with affection and respect, but neither emotional intimacy nor sexual passion.

I will ask him to need me with the heart of the little boy in the playpen. And he, understandably, will refuse. Why should he risk the pain? He has gained a certain maturity; does not blame his parents as a child would; understands their oppression, their youth, the vicissitudes of racism. Why should he become a child again? He is a good man, a strong man, everyone says so.

Why do I torment him, trying to force his walls down, what do I want of him?

I am trying to preserve the friendship we have created over the twelve years we have lived together, birthed children together, grown up together—and add to that friendship the passion of the Shameless Hussy. I am asking him to recognize her, to love her, to answer her ridiculous, childish, ever deepening vulnerability with his own.

Reasonably, he will say no.

And so there is a desert between us across which the Shameless Hussy cries in pain, reaching out for a little boy who hurts so much more than she does that his cries can no longer be heard at all.

5
The Lost Brother/
The Twin

The phantom of the man-who-would-understand,
the lost brother, the twin—

—Adrienne Rich,
"Natural Resources"

1

There are times in my life when nothing proceeds
except by inches. I can easily become impatient with the
stages of change. They are so immune to conscious control, to desire or will. I wish to be serenely integrating new
aspects of my identity into an older, more confident self, or
for a sudden, searing, irreversible insight—I want to believe that the Shameless Hussy, while as passionate as
ever, is domesticated this time, obedient.

Instead I feel like my two young sons who, every few
months, just before they are about to take some important
step away from me, just as they are able to achieve some
new and crucial separation of the self, live through a regression to an earlier stage which is as painful for the rest

of the family as it is for themselves. One becomes defiant and challenging to an unbearable degree; the other becomes physically wild, tearing through the house at each frustration, knocking plates to the floor, bumping into furniture, fighting with other children. In each case, the child exhibits his most characteristic behavior of anxiety, of anger, of frustration. At each new stage the regression is the same in its essential character as all the regressions before.

And then, suddenly, there is growth. The child has changed a bit, has changed unmistakably, has moved a new small step away from parental protection, and he is calm again.

Just as I am reeling from the initial consciousness of my growing separation from James—the recognition that we are not eternally connected by the visible link of our children's beings and their needs, I am thrust back into my own childhood, collecting all the various moments and memories like a beach walker picking up shells. After a while a certain rhythm takes over and you feel as if forced to pick up more and more. Each time one catches your eye you must retrieve it for your already heavily laden pail. An inner voice tells you that you have enough, that you will keep these shells until February and then you will throw them away because you will finally find no use for them, and because, removed from the context of the ocean they will lose their subtlety and brilliance. What seemed a permanent expression of beauty will have become only a reminder, a reflection of what is temporary and irretrievable after all. I collect the moments of my childhood like a beach walker collecting shells, driven by a hypnotic rhythm.

Is it intolerably sad to suggest that perhaps one never

transcends anything? Is it frightening to acknowledge that politics will be betrayed again and again unless they are complex enough to encompass the past as well as the future in ourselves? Is it humiliating to assert, as Dorothy Dinnerstein does in *The Mermaid and the Minotaur*, that "our adult lives resonate with the emotional atmosphere of infancy"?

I collect my memories obsessively. They emerge from the background of my consciousness where they have provided me for a time with the illusion of control, and they loom into full view again—the voices loud, heavy with implication.

There are a few scenes from every childhood that are recaptured with no effort at all. Indeed, they will intrude upon the present moment for reasons that are unclear and inconvenient. They will seem inappropriate because their connection to the present moment is subterranean, intricate. Perhaps I am making love, or I am cooking some complex meal which requires focused attention; I am reading philosophy or writing poetry—and the scene will come upon me. It is a scene which takes all of my childhood, its general character and its particular details, and brings all together in one image—an image which is not merely itself but is magical, a magnetic force drawing many things into itself: a fundamental truth of my life.

The Scene: My father, sad as usual and angry, for some undefined reason, but certainly at his daughters for some sin of omission, some unknown rejection of him, some self-assertion which threatens a betrayal of the Family Trust. (The Family Trust itself is a rather abstract and pervasive notion; my sister and I are always being threatened with losing it, but, like my father's anger, it is

never sufficiently defined.) My father lies on his single
bed, his black clock radio gently pouring Bach into his
one good ear, periodically interrupted by the pretentious
voice of the WQXR announcer. But the volume is turned
way down so that neither the voice nor the music can be
precisely heard; they provide instead only a background
mood: somber, plaintive, even dirgelike. When it gets too
lively he turns it off. But then, he is likely to hear the blast
of Elvis Presley records, and, when he does, he storms
into my room, where he inevitably finds me gyrating wildly
to the music, my facial expression a perfect illustration of
the dangers of loss of reasonable self-control. I am, as
they would say now, turned on. Then we merely called it
hot. I am so involved with my own body that I don't hear
him come in. But—miraculous discrimination of the unconscious mind—I do hear his slight sigh. I feel his ex-
asperation with me as if he had rammed my back with a
log. I feel it so strongly that, as he stands observing me, I
slam the door in his face.

If there had been no sound of Elvis Presley, my father would have continued, in the silence, to read through
every single daily newspaper published in New York City
and a few neighborhood weeklies besides. He reads them
carefully and in a disciplined way, searching not only for
the news—but, dedicated social observer that he is, for
the pulse of the city, and beyond the city, of America
itself. Is street crime increasing, especially against the de-
fenseless elderly? Is the arena of the repercussions of
ghetto poverty, with its cruelties and violence, moving
from Harlem to the South Bronx? What are the implications of these social facts for the working classes solidly
established in this country? And what, twenty years after
his own sacrificial fight for unionism and workers' rights,

is the American worker's vision of the function of the American labor union?

Anyone who is interested in the exploration of these and other related issues cannot read only the *Times*, he has told me with great professorial disdain. So each week he reads the *Post*, the *Amsterdam News*, even the *Daily News*, in his unending quest for Reality, Reality being that aspect of human life which can be defined in a strict, sociological manner, as contrasted to the World of Illusion in which, he warns me, I am in danger of losing my bearings. He means by this my growing interest in psychoanalysis and what he considers to be my obsessive need to draw.

But whatever his judgment upon his daughter's somewhat perturbing interests, here is a man presumably engaged in spending an evening doing as he pleases, doing what it pleases him most to do: studying the world and its events in a way that makes life most comprehensible to him, that takes the confusions and the jarring realities and blends them into an enclosed system with which he is familiar, and in which he passionately believes. Here is a man lying on his bed after a hard day's work, having eaten a fairly pleasant dinner with his children, loosened his shirt and taken off his shoes, relaxing for several hours with the papers and listening to some music.

Then why am I absolutely certain of his fury and of my guilt? For these are the emotions which complete, which in fact characterize the image of my father which comes to me as I am doing the dishes, having just concluded a loud fight with one of my children that then extended itself into a fight with James.

I had been fighting with my older son, who is capable of a good, open fight. He fights with both hands showing. When I yell at him he yells back at me, responding to the content of what I have just said, telling me he thinks me unfair, accusing me of lying, or warning me that I make him want to run away from home. James, on the other hand, never responds to what I say when I raise my voice, but instead begins to fight with me about raising my voice. Even if I lower it and insist that we return to the content of the discussion, he will still only discuss my loudness. That is what has happened tonight. In response to his insistence upon continuing the discussion in this manner, I have banged the dishes around so violently that several of them have broken, including two antique glasses I have just been given by my great aunt that belonged to her mother. And now, as I sweep the pieces up into the pan, I feel, rather than think of, this memory of my father. His silence. His quiet rage. The door to his room seductively opened, the doors to himself slammed shut.

James hates it when I slam doors. I hate it that he is a door-slammer. A door-slammer is someone who slams the door on your hands and then later, when you hold up your bloody fingers saying you have been hurt, says: *Your fingers aren't really bleeding. If they are bleeding a bit, it is yourself who has clumsily slammed the door on them. And besides, what door are you talking about? There was no door.*

I feel my father's door slammed. But when asked directly about his anger, he will say only that he loves me.

Somehow in my search for a maternal man, even in my successful search, for in many ways James is maternal with me, I have preserved in my life that precious, tyrannical quality of my father's.

I slammed the bedroom door on him, shutting out the rustling of his papers, the sound of his mournful music, the sight of his self-righteous mouth. I slam the door today. In the moment of the slamming of the door, in the breaking of a dish, in the wild and unself-conscious dance, I find something that I have repeatedly relinquished.

Retaining the spirit of my father, I grew more and more comfortable with door-slammers. They intrigued me, drew me, attracted me again and again. It was quite simple. I sought them in order to continue the work that has become so habitual over the years: the work of breaking down and pushing open doors.

I bowed to the view that I was so wild that without a few slammed doors around I would invite God knows what into the house. This highly functional self-deprecation matched up like a puzzle piece with my need to love someone who would help me create boundaries by never coming too close.

Soon my memories began to sacrifice a bit of their intensity again. Pulling away, trying to relinquish my love for the door-slammers, I stood like my young children, a bit more alone. It seemed this changed awareness might provide me only with joy—a certain cleanliness—that I could simply put those old habits away, fold them like treasured mementos and store them in the linen closet to be taken out at a safer time. But it was learning to stop wanting the door-slammers that paved the way for an even more dangerous desire.

When I am recapturing the past, but it is far from integrated into a new layer of self; when its themes, instead, are pulling me backward, forcing me to be wild in much the same way as my younger son; when I am behaving without forethought, carrying the past around with me like a heavy suitcase tied with ropes to my wrists; when I can no longer find the old, comfortable sense of being *James's wife*, when I am quite alone; I read Adrienne Rich's poem, "Natural Resources," which articulates in words more clear and images more heavily laden than those in the most startling dream, what I had been wanting, dreaming, and repeatedly relinquishing all along.

5. The phantom of the man-who-would-understand,
    the lost brother, the twin—

    for him did we leave our mothers,
    deny our sisters, over and over?

    did we invent him, conjure him
    over the charring log,

    nights, late, in the snowbound cabin
    did we dream or scry his face

    in the liquid embers,
    the man-who-would-dare-to-know-us?

6. It was never the rapist:
    it was the brother, lost,

    the comrade/twin whose palm
    would bear a lifeline like our own:

    decisive, arrowy,
    forked-lightning of insatiate desire

    it was never the crude pestle, the blind
    ramrod we were after:

> merely a fellow creature
> with natural resources equal to our own.

By the end of the poem, Rich has asserted her own conviction that the dream of the lost brother is illusion, dangerous fantasy, that "another sort of being" was sharing our beds, a being possessed of a terrible passivity in love, a passivity which we mistake,

> —in the desperation of our search—
> for gentleness
>
> But gentleness is active
> gentleness swabs the crusted stump
>
> invents more merciful instruments
> to touch the wound beyond the wound
>
> does not faint with disgust
> will not be driven off

She marks precisely the points of my enormous disappointment, my chronic loss. Still, I cling to the belief that "the man-who-would-understand," "the comrade/twin" is not an illusion, but only rare.

I read the poem over and over again, focusing on the description of the dream, pushing aside the implication of the inevitable disappointment at its center. I begin to see the promise of his existence in several of the men I know. I resurrect his memory, lubricating that memory with my sexual arousal so that it begins to roam freely, easily, finally obsessively through my mind. I imagine him for so long and so consistently that he becomes dangerously real to me. Into his image I drag all the brothers I have ever known.

I use my friend Judith's brother, Billy. He has always been judged slightly wild by his family, called irresponsible. And in fact, he has been trekking around the world for years, seeking adventure after adventure, playing his guitar, writing novels. I secretly, absurdly, decide that his incessant movement is only the traditional male counterpart of my own habitual lack of serenity. Each time I see him, when he pays a visit to New York, I find him more and more beautiful.

To the outline of Billy's face in my mind, I begin to add well-known brothers I've read about: Charlotte Brontë's brother (she wrote her great works of fiction upon his dead body which, like any cannibal, she devoured). I add George Eliot's brother (she repaid his faithlessness and desertion with an abstract devotion made possible only when she actually abandoned him, so that, loving him from afar, she was able to use her energy to become an artist).

I think of all these brothers for weeks. I read about brothers of sisters wherever I can. I try to turn my older son into a brother although that gets dangerous for him, and so, annoyed by the demands of reality, I tell myself to stop. But then, just one more time, when he is sleeping and safe from me, I sneak into his bed and lie next to him with my feet all the way at the bottom of the bed so that I seem the same height as he is and, for a moment, I wonder: *what if he were my brother?* It isn't hard to imagine since he is my firstborn and as such will always carry the weight of all the members of the family on his aching shoulders. An inescapable fact.

Finally, having achieved the required amount of obsessiveness, I begin to dream about men. Not lovers or other well-known faces, but strange men or boys with faces I have never seen before except for one familiar thing: Perhaps the mouth is the mouth of my mother's family, or the eyes have that slight slant at the edge that my paternal relatives always point to as an indisputable sign of the presence of their genes. After I dream these boy-men a few nights in a row, I realize they are all the same—or perhaps I decide they are all the same. No matter. Now they will become all the same.

He is dark-skinned, like me. But his hair is fair or gray, like my father's. He has a full mustache as my father did in his youth. He is solidly built and wears a crumpled white shirt tucked carelessly into his worn brown pants—the kind I find so attractive when they fold around a man's hips and come smoothly over his ass, accentuating its roundness and barely suggesting the crack between the cheeks. In one dream, he is a fellow student who has found the scholarly texts I have been looking for. We rummage through the index together. (He is wearing a blue lumberjack hat.) In the next dream he is my doctor. I am stricken with a rare virus, the chief symptom of which is that I can in no way communicate with the outside world. My body is paralyzed, my speech garbled because of the strange brain fever. I brush my cheek along his thigh as he stands by my bed. He bends down over my terrified face and swears to devote his life to finding a cure for my virus. The thought goes through my mind that without this man I would be lost forever.

What am I seeking in this brother I imagine, dream, and then predictably find? Is it, as Simone de Beauvoir suggests, a traditional case of the aggressive little girl for whom becoming a little boy is the only pathway to recognized, validated strength? Is it some leftover oedipal anxiety struggling to reenact itself in a provocative sort of incestuous desire, as a Freudian would have it? Or am I encountering that male principle deep within myself which, when released, will fertilize my feminine creativity into a thousand, potential-filled buds? I search among the languages of my generation which claim to describe the workings of the interior world. But none of them can fully capture the intensity, the deep relief I feel when I am in the original throes of a passion for a man who seems, for a moment, to be that very brother whose existence my reason has warned me again and again to deny.

2

It was inevitable that I would find him, that I would test myself. Not in a conscious sense, as though I were proceeding toward some clearly defined goal—a female hero in not so shiny armor anxious to prove the strength and tenacity of her internal muscles; but rather a movement toward experience of the sort that propels you and seems to obliterate the power of choice—that is what you tell yourself—when the truth is that you have already chosen.

I see a man and the first time I see him, he cries in public. We are sitting in a room full of people who have come together to discuss their work. We are all writers. We are here to read, to criticize, to dare to speak of the intricate interconnections between the rhythms of our work and the rhythms of our lives. But it is David who dares to speak first because, he says bluntly, he is going through hell. Either he has to speak about his real feelings or he has to leave.

He is tall and his hair is black, curly, and unkempt.

His shirt is plaid, which seems important since it reminds me of a childhood preference. I always liked plaid shirts on boys. His arms are long as are his hands and fingers, and he uses them—fingers, hands, and arms—to articulate that content of his passion which is not expressible in words. He leans forward, looking at each of us, then into space. When he pauses, his arms rest on his knees, his hands hanging over—suggesting hopelessness and fear.

The others, fearful of dissolving the neat dividing lines between their passions and their work, simply watch him. I sit in the room, and I watch him cry. He cries shamelessly. But more than that, he confesses explicit details of his sadness and his loneliness, never retreating into a distancing generalization. It would be so easy to say: I am very unhappy in my life and this prevents me from working well. Instead he explains that he has recently separated from his wife and small child. He yearns for them. He describes his rage, his long-buried hurt. He talks of sudden impotence, of unreturned desire, of his still persisting love for a woman who has scratched his ego into a disintegrated oblivion. But there is something in the way he reveals himself that enlarges rather than diminishes him, and his vulnerability does not create a sense of shame as it can when it is sentimental and inauthentic. On the contrary, it makes him seem proud.

He describes the agony of living with his three-year-old boy only half the week. He describes his growing knowledge that his wife did not love him the way he had forced himself to believe she did, recounts the years during which he buried the rage implicit in that knowledge until he had found a way to blame himself for her many rejections, the countless times he had convinced himself that it was he who wanted too much, who demanded too much, who was too needy, a leftover child in the awkward body of a man.

I think: If I were talking to his wife I would hear another story. For I am certain there is another story to tell. And yet this person—he happens to be a man—is telling a side of the story with which I can thoroughly identify. I sympathize as I would with any woman who revealed herself so completely.

Suddenly he looks up at us all and asks genuinely, "Is this all right? Am I making you angry or uncomfortable?"

He has made me neither angry nor uncomfortable. He has made my pants soaking wet in the crotch.

There is something in the ability to reveal self to self alone and only by chance to whomever is listening and to do so suddenly, as if there is no choice, no conscious decision, but rather an eruption of inner necessity, that I find literally irresistible in men and in women.

I remember teaching a class in women's studies once, on the theme of woman as hero, and discussing, in the first session, the complex layers of a felt identity, the way a conviction about who one is, felt with great certainty, can fold into doubt as soon as it is spoken, the moment another possibility, even a contradictory one, asserts itself.

"What would you say, most immediately, to the question, 'Who are you?'" I asked, afraid that no one at all would answer, or that the answers would be thoroughly reductive, *My name is* . . . and my carefully dramatized point thus lost. But a young woman raised her hand, brushed her long black hair away from her eyes, wiggled around in the seat a little, pulling her hands out of her dungaree pockets and readying them for assertive point making, and said, "I am a poet. I am a Dominican. I am a woman. I am a lesbian. I am here in this class thinking maybe I can make it in college after several false starts. I am above all a musician."

I thought right then that I would come to love her, and I have.

The roots of my passion and of my friendship with David grew on precisely the same spot of ground.

We are walking on a beach and talking of our immediately felt sense of kinship—therein lies the double satisfaction: not only do we experience the sense of connection but, both of us talkers, we articulate the connection out loud.

We are connected in several major ways. We are both writers. His father, like mine, was a dedicated Communist, although from a slightly different tradition. While mine was a working-class organizer, uneducated in formal American terms, his was a theoretician and an academic, a teacher of Marxist philosophy, more rigid than my father in his emotional expression, but less pure in his ideological consistency. David had the precision, the humor, the conviction of his Communist father, but he also had the chaotic wildness, the unrealistic hopefulness of the Communist child. And, though I could not have known it that afternoon on the beach, it was precisely the way in which David was both my father and myself that made him seem the perfect comrade of my soul.

As we walk down the beach, close to the water, I am infatuated with his playfulness and irresponsibility, possessed by his abandon. As we talk, I realize that five years before I would have told myself that I could never love such a man on the grounds that he was too much like myself.

"Sometimes when I'm working on a piece of writing," he says, "I am actually aware that I'm covering over a part of myself—the part of me that needs anything from anyone. And each time I feel the covering over there is a sort of cowardly relief. I know how to do it automatically, maybe because I'm a man."

I am quick to admit my envy, how I long to acquire this masculine ability, this long-held male prerogative. I am struggling to develop the habit of doing just what he is able to do so automatically: to protect my core in an ability to work, to draw boundaries, to hold myself momentarily apart through a commitment to something other than love.

He tells me about his father—at once adored and resented; the way he always seemed to disapprove of him, of his interests; the way he always seemed more heroic than David could ever be. I begin to tell him about the Shameless Hussy, but he knows her already, predicts all her immoderate behavior, describes each antisocial desire she has given in to with a wonderful accuracy.

And then we are holding each other, hugging each other's bodies. In that tight, still embrace, each holds safely for a moment the need to express the self to another, to feel completely understood. As I stand there in his arms, the sand blowing around my feet, the graceful and slender teenagers walking by us, either oblivious to or tolerant of this older man and woman in their midst, I suddenly remember a moment in my childhood when I experienced intense isolation, and the memory of this old feeling—the perfect antithesis to what I feel now—peels

away whatever layers of protection against vulnerability I
still possess.

I am on a camp bus, no more than nine years old. I
am new in the camp, and the girls in my group are all ten
and eleven. I am too young for the older group and too
old for the younger group—naturally there was no doubt
in my father's mind as to which group I belonged in. I sit
in the back of the bus on the way to the lake, on the way
to the baseball games, on the way to hiking spots, always
in the back of the bus, and I watch. The few girls and
boys with whom I wish to be friends, who are the most
popular kids in the camp, sit right in front of me. The
boys are from the oldest group—they are thirteen, practi-
cally men. They are so involved in their flirtations, their
teasing sexuality, that they do not notice that I am always
staring. For days I stare in order to understand their rules,
hoping futilely that sooner or later one of the boys will
turn around and flirt with me. Of course I have already
picked out the one I like. He is the most sought-after boy
in the entire camp. All of the thirteen-year-old girls like
him, but I know from my obsessional observations that he
likes one of the eleven-year-olds in my group. Now they
are playing a game in which they try to guess the girl he
wants for his summer girlfriend. They are naming all of
the thirteen-year-old girls, the ones whose breasts are already somewhat developed, whose hips come out from
indisputable waists, whose delicate gray underarm shadows indicate that they have been shaving their armpits for
several months at least. And in the locker room, when we
all undress together for swimming, I have noticed that
their pubic hair is full and lush, creeping slightly down the
insides of their thighs, while the other ten-year-olds and I

are lucky if we have a thin line of hair growing alongside the crack. Still, with the special advantage of the audience, I have watched him watch the other girls. I view all the actors at once, understand their relation to each other, mark the secret movements which are hidden from the other principals, which are even at times unconscious to the self. I know that he likes Barbara, an eleven-year-old.

Toby, someone guesses, and he responds with a seductive, *No*.

Ellen, says another, in a voice full of anxiety because Ellen is the well-known girlfriend of the handsomest and strongest boy in camp. They think; they pause. The game is played carefully, the guessing itself becoming an irresistible flirtation for the girls who wish to identify the mysterious woman, for the boy who keeps their undivided attention as long as he keeps them in ignorance.

What gave me the courage, the impudence, the pride to interrupt at that point and declare, *I know who it is?*

All the insiders turn to me, the new girl in the backseat, staring at them knowledgeably, foolishly assuming that the answer to the question is actually the point of the discussion and insisting that she, virtually nonexistent in the social hierarchy of the camp, knows the girlfriend who is sitting nearby, within earshot, no doubt desperately eager to be named.

And then, *Barbara*, I say proudly, without the slightest trivializing smile.

The girls stare at me in disbelief. The boy, whose face now seems handsomer than ever, whose eyes meet mine for a glorious moment as I seem to read his mind, says in a quiet and shocked tone: *Yes, she's right*. Then he looks over shyly at Barbara whose nose and mouth are pasted to the window but whose shoulders mark the posture of someone in rapt attention, someone who has not missed a word.

"How did she know?" the boy asks the electrified air between his eyes and Barbara's turned back. Within the next few minutes he moves over next to her. He is the most popular boy in camp. He needn't wonder long whether he will be rebuffed. Soon they are holding hands.

The others continue to look at me periodically during the bus ride, as if I were some mysterious witch with magical powers, not understanding from their position on center stage how ridiculously easy it is from the outside to perceive the undercurrents of action that can seem so confusing to those who participate in a direct way.

I, of course, feel no great fulfillment as a result of my proven powers of observation. It is Barbara's hand that is being held. I am still in the backseat, odder than ever before.

Now, held by someone neither fearful of nor infatuated with my difference but rather, like Joey, effortlessly comfortable with my familiarity, standing on that beach, we are sister and brother. We cannot let go of each other. There is no kiss, no attempt at sexual touching. We are hugging as I have seen my sons do after a long period of unrelenting rivalry, the embrace symbolizing their everlasting connection: They have lain for nine months within the same womb. Their features and personalities, no matter how different they are perceived to be within the confines of a small family, are still more like each other's than like any other being's in the world.

Like my two small sons, we hug to rid ourselves for

as long a moment as possible of enforced solitude, of deserts. The Shameless Hussy, her pride not required for a restorative moment, cries.

Is this what the psychoanalysts mean when they talk of *merging*? Is this complete identification, this restorative sense of thorough acceptance what I have so come to fear?

Is Lily Briscoe, to the degree that she lives within me holding high a beacon of separateness and autonomy, is she a dead duck if I succumb to the temptations of such an unbounded love? Or am I, after all these years per-haps, capable of drawing my own boundaries in response to my own needs rather than in a required response to the needs of another?

Might I achieve with a man the easy intimacy I have come to love with women, or will it finally be sex that precludes the survival of Lily Briscoe in the same body as the Shameless Hussy?

I would like to be able to write an ordinary love story, full of the rhythms of joy, conventional in structure, a story with a beginning, a middle, an end. Its integrating theme would be the exhilaration of discovering the exis-tence of a man who seemed to match me in every way. Instead I must write of my own passion, because that is what I was left with—a story of that particularly female experience which we all use to balance the scales against our many losses; the experience we desperately cling to as the Giver of Meaning in those moments of abandonment when life and its persistence seem most absurd: the tena-cious promise of internal growth.

And yet how many times I wished to sacrifice the growth, to relinquish without qualm or regret further *understanding of the self*—how I was even willing to thoroughly abandon my self, while another part of me, intact yet powerless, watched my behavior in stunned amazement. I wished to be the woman whom he needed too much to leave forever, the woman to whom he felt so unalterably connected that their parting filled him with stark terror; I longed to be her, the one to whom he felt ties that, however frayed by rage and chronic loneliness, would prove inexorable, irrevocable, deeper by far than ties of love.

Whatever carefully considered opinions I possessed regarding the possible existence of *the lost brother*, whatever sense of balance sustained by any healthy, cynical realism I could claim in the face of immense sexual passion, however I might have feared, even then, that no man—not yet—could share with me the intimate depths that were reached so easily with women friends, all of this was met with a strong dose of simple leftover romanticism when I first knew David. It seemed wonderfully simple for a while. A mixture of passion and friendship that no one in her right mind could turn down.

Who he was; his history; his dark black hair; his somewhat unconcerned way of dressing—as if he were embarrassed to adorn his confident body that had been carefully created over years in the pursuit of grace and control; the particular way he cried, not "like a man" but sobbing from his guts as if he suddenly viewed his entire being without defense, with a merciless transparency—all these seemed to be of central importance. I felt myself to be a wanderer moored finally not to just any rock but to the only rock in the ocean that could have saved me. I lived for his presence.

The passion finally was enormous. It was uncontainable. I would have sacrificed everything in its pursuit: peace of mind, friendship, work. I would have lain on the floor, waiting until he asked me to rise, I would have chained him to my bed, kept him there, always in sight, knowing that whenever I wished to touch him, to be touched by him, there he would be.

I had imagined making love to him a dozen times, a hundred times. I knew that he would sense my needs, that our needs would meet. Only fools can imagine that sexual power is a matter of technique. We loved each other with our bodies from the start. His movements occasionally reminded me of my father. A tone of voice would recall an old memory of my mother—a sense of acceptance. The heavy line he always drew between his desires and his obligations, and yet the passion to integrate the two, re-minded me of myself. When we made love the tension between the difficulties of the present and the intense rich-ness of an insurmountable past simply crumbled. At first there was nothing more than that new, startling fact of life.

It was not "merely sex"—if there is such a thing. I experienced sex in a way that reminded me of the girl of fifteen hiding on the roof from Mr. Nash—filled with the most complex associations, my most precious secret needs suddenly erupting into consciousness. It was clear that the Shameless Hussy was no longer a girl but had grown up right along with me.

I have never met a woman who experiences sexuality in this depth within a marriage of ten years or more, no matter how much passion she may feel for her husband, no matter with what empathy and precision they have come to know each other's physical needs. It was simply a different order of experience—one that I will never

banish from my life so long again. I have no idea how to
integrate this insight with the demand for loyalty, the need
for abiding relationship that must often be based on
exclusivity when sexuality is involved, the destructiveness
of lying to a person whom you love and live with and to
whom you are unalterably committed in friendship; and
yet the equally intense destruction of allowing him to live
with the knowledge that you are involved passionately
with someone else. I don't know how to untangle the
threads of personal need, obligation to others, stage of
life; the demands of self-creation from the dangers of risking all that makes one feel secure, safe, enclosed in a
harbor that has always felt like a port of home. I only
know that for a time my passion felt like the only way I
could recognize and reassert some long-buried part of myself, and as such it required a ruthless dedication to my
own needs. Yet, at the same time, it included a most dangerous kind of self-denial—the kind that involves a re-
duction of the self to one aspect, so that at the same moment as I felt enhanced I also felt frighteningly diminished,
as if I had utterly lost the ability to make decisions fed by
the broadest considerations of my life. Instead, I moved
as if determined by a force that only seemed to be external because it was so irresistible; in fact that force drew
its power from the earliest layers of my consciousness.

This loss of the broader self may inevitably accompany certain kinds of passion for both men and women.
But for reasons that seem obvious, the situation is particularly dangerous for women. The danger lies in the clash
between the personal search for the self and political reality.

In *The Second Sex*, Simone de Beauvoir analyzes, in
painfully familiar detail, the "woman in love," *l'amoreuse*.

She unconsciously, repeatedly, and unequivocally com-
promises her sense of autonomy; she desires to bind a man
to her through a combination of childbearing and domesticity; her interest in work, if she has developed such an
interest to begin with, diminishes into lethargic, grandiose
fantasies. If he leaves her, she feels she will go mad, for
she feels herself to be alive only in the presence of the
adored man. This is our history—the one we hear confessed to us by every woman to whom we come close
enough to share confessions (and women easily share
confessions about love), revealed by even those women
who seem the most autonomous, the most developed in
their work—in their lives. When the talk turns to passion,
all of them confess the same experience. He took over my
life. When he left me (and they usually leave) I had to
crawl on my bloody hands to the surface again.

The desire, the heroic urge, to describe and reveal
the painful, often humiliating details of these experiences,
has informed several recent books by women writers.
Nine and a Half Weeks, written under the name Elizabeth
McNeill, a pseudonym, and the novel *Bad Connections*,
by Joyce Johnson, tell the story of such passions, the story
of a dangerous and intoxicating loss of self. One deals
with a short, brutal love affair characterized by the most
frightening kind of sadomasochism enacted upon the
body of the woman. The other deals with a longer, more
conventional affair in which, however, the brutality of the
man is just as dehumanizing, his desire for power as complete. But what is important and heroic about both these
books is that the writers sought the ultimate cause of the
woman's subservience in the woman herself. The desire to
submit, the overwhelming willingness to relinquish auton-

omy, to become the slave and object of a man, is linked up with the most intense sort of sexual desire. Both books end with the woman's reclamation of self, but not in a powerful surge of autonomy or pure insight; rather in a small, almost imperceptible step toward the regaining of power. The woman who has been physically brutalized breaks down, and in the utter passivity of illness she rediscovers the boundaries of her still existing but pale and disappointingly ordinary self. The woman whose life has been taken over by a selfish and ungiving man simply gets on a plane one day and goes away, not really planning to leave him—nothing so conscious or strong—just, for the moment, leaving. Both women describe their lives in the last pages of their books as better, stronger, but dull—characterized by a gray mediocrity that is impossible to dissipate and yet which protects, heals, even nourishes.

Tillie Olsen, in a letter to me, distinguished between descriptions of women in love that accept "the old constriction to one dimension; confinement to biological as male-defined, sex-partner woman," and books that explore "the truth about the body . . . [we must] separate [our] hatred of this exploitation of 'love' to coerce women,—from the need, power, legitimacy of writing of this most profound, consequential emotion . . ."

These two books should be considered examples of the second sort of story, testimonies to the important piece of knowledge that, no matter how creative and filled with pleasure and depth a passionate relationship with a man may be, there is this other thing, this not yet understood link between enormous passion and the willingness, the need, to obliterate the self, to let go the reins in a long moment of magnificent powerlessness, and that the desire for powerlessness may fuse and intensify the passion. Even in the midst of the paradoxical obliteration and adoration of the self that passion involves, a man is not likely to so completely lose his moorings: he has responsibilities that are both internally unquestioned and validated in the external world. There are probably several people dependent upon him, upon his work, upon his earning capacities, upon his psychic strength in the face of crisis. And as a result of these long-nurtured psychic habits, he does not as easily lose his connection to the demands of work, which will enable him not to transcend the self-involvement of passion altogether, but perhaps to contain it.

And yet, the easy transformation into *l'amoreuse* is not merely a case of traditional female masochism, although it may include a dose more or less of that. I gloried in the powerful feeling of giving pleasure as much as I yearned for the opposite feeling—to utterly submit to the eye, the hand, the body of another. There was no desire to be hurt or to hurt, rather to assert the self, and to submit, alternately, shamelessly, with dignity and care. It seemed at times as if David were the only human being in the world who could call forth these feelings in me.

He had a wildness, a tendency to be outrageous, that restored my self-respect. I once saw him try to prove a point about the basic virtue of the human body. We were at a large family picnic, many adults slightly high, many children of all ages crawling and running around, the babies even sitting on top of the old wooden picnic table, poking into the grown-ups' plates as we ate. Suddenly an eighteen-month-old child standing on the table spread her legs and peed a small puddle right next to the barbecued spare ribs. Confronted with the squeamishness of several of the guests, and before the mother of the child could wipe up the urine, David grabbed a piece of french bread, used it to sop up the piss, and ate it.

A few people gagged good-naturedly, providing him with his audience. Others grumbled at his grandiosity, calling him offensive, certain that he was mocking them. Many, reading this description, might find themselves revolted, certain that the incident would repel any woman with even a minimal degree of sanity. But for me the incident was a perfectly drawn metaphor of the paradox at the center of the attraction I felt to David. While his intensity and uncontrolled impulsiveness would have terrified me several years before, now I gloried in his excess, for if I loved it so much in him I was close to admitting that I valued it in myself, was even willing to sacrifice to its continued development that dubious, tantalizing, and impossible prize I had pursued for so long—the approval of everyone in the world. I began to talk as loudly as I wanted to and as often, always imagining David in the back of my mind, applauding—and he confessed he did the same with me. The point, of course, is not in the value of intensity or outrageousness as aspects of character, but that what had been buried in each of us, what felt at once most authentic and yet most prohibited in each of our histories, was very much the same. Loving that quality in each other was a prelude to an acceptance of the self.

Over several months I began to relinquish the collection of people I had always gathered around me who used me to dramatize their own unexpressed urges and deepest needs. My friendship with David had gone so deep that the thankless task of pushing open slammed doors which had seemed so heroic to me, filled with a determined innocence, now seemed idiotic, absurd. It felt so good to rush through an open door and have someone waiting right behind it, rushing toward you, clumsily and anxiously crashing into your body as he reached out to grab you close to his own.

David was then living through a short period in his life when he reveled in the very impulses he had always been taught to despise. Eventually he would use these impulses only to prove to himself that, without any parental prodding, he had the self-possession to keep them under control, the very intensity of his impulses attesting to the value of the self-denial. He would leave me long before I was ready to let him go, leave me to return to his family, his marriage of opposites. He was afraid, he said, of the feelings our connection called up in him, and afraid of my desperate willingness to follow those feelings wherever they might go. He left so fast, with such a frightened eagerness, that I hardly had the chance to wonder if I would have left my family for him. But I wondered for many months about the painful diversity in the ways people change, the way two people can meet for a long moment in which their needs seem identical, when suddenly there is a fork in the road, and what seemed an utter mutuality of purpose turns out instead to be only a momentary convergence, transitory and confusing, and what seemed a promise for the future turns instead into an engulfing recollection of the past.

It is the early morning. My children have gone to school, my husband to work. Six months before I would have "gone to work" as well—sat down at my desk and began. I would have had my day either planned or carefully unplanned so that I could write.

Now I am no longer a mature woman with children,

with work, with a home; I do not feel as if the rest of my life awaits my attention. I feel as if my entire life has been unbelievably drained of meaning if I cannot have this man whom I have known for six months. For months each morning after my family have gone off to their own lives I go to mine—the life of mourning, of weeping uncontrollably, of filling up volumes of journals with a repetitive, intricate record of my pain. I walk up and down the streets because only that physical movement will ease the terrible anxiety which is unassuaged by the compassion of friends, by the arms of my children, by tranquilizing pills. I walk my mornings away until they are afternoons, up and down the drive near the river, wishing it were time to pick up my children from school. It is only months later that I will see that I mourn many deaths.

One morning I am writing in my journal, crying as usual, wondering if I will ever piece myself together again, amazed that I have been so undermined and unbalanced by this loss, and I begin to call for David out loud. I begin to feel myself lose control, I cross a certain boundary which feels familiar to me, a place where I leave behind the desire for control, where I instantaneously, almost without will, make the decision to discover what wild, irrational feelings exist over the line. And I go there, into the feelings which are usually kept just out of reach, the feelings which I keep penned in with my activities, with physical exertion, with fatigue, with sleep. But now they are here, surrounding me. My adulthood hangs formlessly just near the window sill, one of those veils that can seem so perfectly authentic at another time and now seems completely illusory, a costume one dons for a party. *A child calls the name of David and cries and screams until an image floods her mind. A baby*

is screaming in a crib. The face of the baby is the face of
my younger child, of my little boy, standing in the crib,
clutching the bars, throwing his body against the side,
calling me. He has been crying for an hour, and I cannot
bear to answer him. Or I feel he needs to cry out his
tension so that he will finally sleep. Or he has been crying
so long that day that I am immobilized by anger. Or I just
don't know what to do. But I don't go to him. I listen to
him cry. When I finally go to pick him up, he keeps calling
Mommy while he holds me, he calls *Mommy* as if I am
not yet there, while he wraps his legs and arms around my
body, clutching me, pasting himself to me, trying to put
me back together with his mommy who would not leave
him alone so long.

*The child calls the name of David until it becomes
the word Mommy. She calls it, that long unused word,
that word she has now herself become, but has not used
out loud calling another in thirty years. She calls and
calls, feeling relieved as if she has been gently opened
with a delicate razor so that all the pent-up pain can pour
out, feeling afraid as if one more moment of this intensity
may destroy the boundaries of her body while all the pent-
up pain pours out. Feeling relieved, feeling afraid, as if
she has at last broken through to the land Death stretch-
ing out behind the dark green portrait and still she is
surrounded by silence, as if no one is there.*

The moment when the call for David and the call for
mother become one returns again and again for many
months. Each time I think it's over, that I have reclaimed
for good my veil of adulthood and will not become a
small child again, each time I think the ghosts of my par-

ents have been banished a final time, they come back, demanding to be abandoned again. The veil slips off, and if I cannot bear the strength of that perfectly entangled fusion I run to the drive near the river and walk the afternoon away until it is time to pick up my children.

That time of unbearable anxiety, when past and present losses dangerously merged, passed eventually, and an old rationality gradually returned. I resisted that rationality because of the grayness it brought in its wake; I welcomed it because it included the other parts of my life which I still loved but which I had somehow temporarily forgotten. I tried to discover why what was potential had not become actual with David, why our shared connection was a force from which he ultimately fled. I cannot yet find my way through the complex overlapping of truths. And I am not yet certain whether I am left with rage or disappointment, realism or cynicism, a fear of men and of love given new tenacity by a rejection far more mature and conscious than Colin O'Connor's, or reawakened hope in the possibility, at least, of an authentic connection between a man and a woman. I am left with only one indisputable piece of knowledge, at once deeply ironic and sustaining because it restates in a new way an older, more traditional truth. I feel as an undeniable almost physical presence the common root of my need for a comprehensive intimacy and my desire for sex.

It would be convenient, modern, and in accordance with both popular and scholarly wisdom to say, from an attractive distance, that I learned from the pain of my separation from David that each human being is finally alone. That in recapturing my loves and losses through him I buried my parents and their legacy a final time. That I discovered it was only myself who would be strengthened by the passion, the abundance, the individuality of the Shameless Hussy: that there are no external twins. That in my search for a center from which the self might act, I achieve a certain peace derived from my acceptance that certain needs can never be fully answered, not by James, not by a woman, not by David, not even by a remote and glorified mother of my infancy. That in combining for myself a life involved with description through words, a work that seeks to unify political commitment with aesthetics, I incorporate the best of my father's gift to me, and in reclaiming the Shameless Hussy I begin the work of banishing his various accusations, silencing his voice.

It would not only be convenient, it would also be true to assert that I have learned again that I am alone, that the Shameless Hussy will live on, despite my unfulfilled longing for her reflection in David's eyes, that like Lily Briscoe I must relentlessly force myself to keep a part of my energy separate from men, because of their power, because of their capacity to reach into my core—that the time has not yet come when I can completely trust myself to remain intact in the presence of love. That like Hester Prynne, that wise old slut, I do in the end value growth as a Giver of Meaning.

It would be convenient as well as true to say that my love for James has become as unending and indescribable as my love for my parents, my sister, my sons. And that at the same time it might be absolutely necessary at some time for us to part, because what I no longer wish for is his parental protection—the sturdy, supportive, wonderfully precious security of a slammed door.

And yet, though all this is both wise and true, I have learned something about the powerful restoration of the spirit and the intellect that comes from a union with a person like myself—with a man who can understand. If we are each finally alone, it is also possible to achieve moments of intimacy with another which nourish solitude and ease loss.

Perhaps, as Adrienne Rich asserts, the *lost brother* does not exist. But I experienced through the intensity of my short connection to David the certainty that he can. That may be the poison at the center of the dream—not that it can never be true, for that would mercifully extinguish the hope, but that it is *not yet true*; not that the *lost brother* does not exist, but that potentially at least he does.

I understand the broader themes that give a context to my personal confusion best through women's literature and art, and I know only in a general sense that these themes indicate a change in me that I cannot yet fully articulate.

In college I was taught how to analyze literature. I was taught the logic of combining a knowledge of the historical period in which a work was written with a knowledge of the basic elements of prose style and with a familiarity with the symbolic potential of, for example, Christian or psychoanalytic mythology. It was for this reason that I gave up the study of literature as a profession. Because that other thing involved in the study of literature—the identification between myself and what I was reading—always took over for me to such a degree that I could not even remember central facts if that last element were not there. It was Mr. Stringboch and the math book all over again, and I couldn't seem to learn, once and for all, that the easiest way to ward off criticism and humiliation was not to reveal yourself. Thus, upon reading *The Plague* by Albert Camus, for the first time, and encountering all those literal and symbolic rats, I revealed to my classmates my near-hallucinatory rat obsession, which had plagued me since the age of ten, wondering aloud if my unconscious and Camus's had anything in common. Next, instead of analyzing Lady Brett Ashley in reasonable tones, with instances from the text to prove my point that she was utterly unlike any woman I had ever known, that she talked like a man, swigged scotch like a man, loved like a man, I fought against her as if she were a living adversary in such passionate terms that instead of considering my points everyone began talking about why I was so upset.

But when I read *To the Lighthouse* and came to the final vow between sister and brother to resist the tyranny of the father, I was not attending school. I was grappling with the contradictions between marriage and autonomy. I was trying to understand something about intimacy and friendship on the one hand, passion and desire on the other. I was trying to figure out why the connection to the lost brother appeared to be so ephemeral—so frightening. And I had no one to obey.

I had read of the son, Oedipus, killing his father. I had read of the father, Agamemnon, killing the daughter, Iphigenia. Of the wife, Clytemnestra, killing her husband, Agamemnon. And of the son, Orestes, killing the mother, Clytemnestra. Nowhere had I read of the daughter killing her father. Why had this murder not taken place in literary history?

Cam, the sister, in the last section of *To the Lighthouse*, proves unable to accomplish this symbolic task. She relinquishes the promise of autonomy by succumbing to daughterhood a final time. For diluting her rage at her father's absolute power is the exquisite, irresistible desire to be protected by him.

"You're not exposed to it," she thinks of her brother, "this pressure and division of feeling, this extraordinary temptation."

She recalls her luxurious thoughts, seated in the study while the old men are reading *The Times*: "Now I can go on thinking whatever I like, and I shan't fall over a precipice or be drowned, for there he is, keeping his eye on me."

Like Cam, I am pervaded by the temptation to remain the daughter of a father. I lie on the bed while James reads his paper or watches the basketball game on TV. I do not experience a trace of insomnia. I do not listen for footsteps at the door. I imagine no rapists on the stairwell. I think whatever seductive thoughts come to mind. I sleep.

The brother, of course, may weaken too. Cam's brother, James, weakens through a moment of identification with his father—a connection that he experiences as their shared loneliness—the loneliness of the masculine priority, of patriarchal responsibility, the loneliness of the tyrant whether he is beneficent or cruel, and symbolized by the actual lighthouse, which is neither lovely nor elegant as "the ladies" had imagined viewing it from afar. Rather it is "a stark tower on a bare rock."

And suddenly the fury of the brother, of the son, is transformed into sympathy. He is to become the father—protecting, earning money, standing between the harsher realities of the world and the women and children. Both daughter and son have been defeated, although the bribes have been very different. Only Lily, back on shore,

achieves her moment of autonomy, of full consciousness
—what Virginia Woolf called elsewhere her "moment of
being"—and Lily Briscoe is alone.

But supposing I make another choice? Seeing the
obvious fact that the tyrant remains a tyrant in part because I need him to, supposing I confirm my rebellion by
asserting out loud the impotence of that old man, sitting
in the stern, reading his book, mumbling about how we
are all ultimately alone? Imagine I am willing to transform my rebellion into an authentic discovery of the self
and collaborate with my brother to the end? Supposing
Cam, taking oar, agrees to turn the boat away from the
hated lighthouse and asks her brother to keep faith with
her rebellious pact?

The brother may agree. But if he does, he gives up
something more than his sister. He gives up the power,
however stark and lonely, of the patriarch, and the internal sense of potency and identity, however tenuous,
that comes along with the prize.

If he is afraid, his fear reciprocates my own. We are
both afraid, and so in our opposites we find security.
Having been taught to believe we are unacceptable, we
dutifully hope that in loving someone who represents
everything we are not, we will assume control over everything we are. And we acquiesce to the belief that it is our
truest selves that may potentially destroy all those we love.

By expressing my sexuality I humiliate my father. By
a primary commitment to work I abandon my children.
By trying to discover myself I must forego dignity and
pride.

I was not fully conscious of the lie of these assertions
when, at fifteen, I lay on the bed, confused and frightened, having been vilified as a slut by Gerald Burman. I

am still often prone to forget they are lies. But I know now that the inescapable relationship, which I merely sensed then, between my consciousness of my own sexuality and my ability to create lies here: both require an absolute assertion of the self. Neither can be achieved without the integration of the Shameless Hussy.

The risk of loving the *lost brother*, of acknowledging the man who is like myself, is a desire rooted in the creative urge to change—to transcend the traditional *woman in love* who seeks in sexuality the father, to whom she must submit, or the son, whom she must control. To give up the search for connection, no matter how thankless it may prove to be, is to deny my passion, to betray my power, to abandon my sons.

6
Mother
and Son

I say:
you shall be a child of the mother as of old, and your face
will not be turned from me . . .

—Robin Morgan, "The Child,"
Part IV of "The Network of the Imaginary Mother"

1

Last summer I was climbing a rather high mountain
of dirt that bordered a pond. I was climbing with my
friend Judith and her two-year-old daughter, Emma. A
sturdy, brazen and physically strong little girl, Emma
climbed ahead of us up the slippery mud. I reached for
her ankles, afraid of the drop into the water below. But
she slithered and kicked away from me. She climbed until
she reached the top. Then, solidly on all fours, she turned
around to us, smiled her widest grin, and yelled,

"Hello down there. I up here!"

As I stood there looking up at that child climbing a
hill I knew that it mattered to me very much that Emma
was a girl. When I saw her clinging proudly to the top

146

of the mud mountain, I completed a cycle in myself that had started right after she was born and I began, with fear and sadness, to understand the difference for me between mothering a son and a daughter. It was an experience during which I achieved a clarity about myself through a clarity about the nature of my connection to my oldest friend.

Judith and I, city bred, sat in the living room of a country house in Connecticut, protected by locked doors and comforted by readied candles, waiting for a hurricane that had been predicted in somber, warning tones since early morning. Several times during the day, we had considered going back to the city. But our husbands, both country boys by birth and upbringing, scoffed. They had lived through storms before, they said. They had watched as the hurricanes of their childhoods had focused their formidable power upon trees and cars and all furniture that was not tied down.

Perhaps we should—they agreed—tie down the heavy furniture, and certainly all yard toys should be put in the garage. "Anything after all can become a lethal weapon in a storm," one of them had coolly advised.

The storm was predicted for 11 P.M. At 10:30, having had a hectic day between the housebound children and the preparations, the men announced they were going to sleep. Judith and I were astonished. Weren't they going to wait for the hurricane? What if it came in their sleep, suddenly knocking a tree into the house? The men laughed and went upstairs where the boys were already sleeping soundly.

Judith and I, partly out of need, partly out of defiance, swore to each other to sit the night out together.

Candles were readily accessible. We had opened the windows slightly as the neighbors had advised. The portable radio, plugged in for the time being, hummed a low buzz on the table.

Two women sat in the country living room, waiting for the storm, talking, reading, and rocking the cradle in which—peacefully for the moment—slept Judith's new baby, a girl at last, named Emma.

Our mothers had been friends in childhood. Now our small sons were friends. On my bookshelf at home I had framed a picture: the grandmothers, the mothers, and then the little children. Three generations of friendships.

Our fathers had also shared a history, had loved each other. And despite the extreme psychological differences between the two, we tended to associate them one with the other, think of them as the same sort of man. At the root of this identification was the fact that we saw ourselves as their spiritual heirs. We thought the influence of our mothers was comparatively remote in our lives. Even now, there was a tendency in us both to relish a kind of regressive journey into the past, discussing our fathers at length, exploring the positive effects of such strong male identification upon the achievements and ambitions of young girls. That night we talked of the connections between politics and literature, trying to make as many bridges as possible between our fathers' passions and our own, enjoying the incestuous implications of having married stable, politically active men.

The thunder began to crack in the heavy, deep blue-black sky. It was almost midnight, but we could still see the low-hanging dark gray clouds wrenched apart by the white streaks of lightning whose power had always been reassuringly domesticated in the city. Suddenly the lights went out and with them the power that kept the radio on. But Judith had forgotten to buy batteries. I teased her about this, threatening to report her to the editors of *Woman's Day* and *Family Circle* for revisionist inefficiency. Defiantly, she lit her candles, giving me a markedly superior look. She, who all her life had been clumsy and disorganized, was now the keeper of a house, the responsible mother of children. She bought candles. She hung curtains. She shopped for food. Only during intimate moments did we admit to each other our shared sense of inadequacy in such matters; our hopeless lack of interest in domesticity. Otherwise, we pretended. What we wanted was that elusive sense we had always sought that we were just like the other girls after all.

The wind was blowing wildly by now; in the yard the weeping willow was swaying in a wide arc so that it looked as if the roots might in fact be pulled out during one of its swings. The rain poured down heavily and came sloshing in through the slightly opened windows. The thunder cracked loudly and Judith, in both mock and authentic terror, raced to the sofa, where she burrowed under a quilt.

Upstairs the little boys and the men slept miraculously unperturbed. Of the children, only Emma, the baby, the first girl, awoke periodically to the crashing of the thunder, and then we would take turns rocking her country, handmade cradle, each thinking of the oddity that we, city girls and Jews, should be sitting here in the middle of this New England storm rocking a beautiful, wooden, handmade cradle, and that we, girls who had always identified with our fathers, should be so moved and perhaps even transformed in some small way by the fact that one of us, at last, was the mother to a baby girl.

Despite the careful rocking of the cradle, Emma began to cry. Judith lifted her and began to nurse her as milk spilled over from her full breasts. And, having nursed two boy babies, I was shocked to find myself filled with an unexpected envy. It was then I saw that I had been quite wrong in my conviction that being a mother to a boy or to a girl would be the same.

The identification with the first child, I had thought, the early sense of its androgyny which can last for several years—these surely prevented any distinction made on the mother's part in response to the sex of the child. But now suddenly I realized that this was false. Watching Judith nurse her daughter I knew with some horror what the difference would be. I asked her, "How do you feel when men friends or even your husband are very needy, I mean when they communicate to you in subtle ways that they need bolstering, uplifting; when they seem to require your attention? When they corner you and seem to say: I am a man. Give to me. How do you feel?"

Judith shuddered. "I resent them. I hate them. Even if I love them, even if I would like to answer their need."

"My father used to ask like that," I said.

But now the baby began to fuss, push the nipple out of her mouth, and Judith's attention was immediately lost to the discussion. She tried to respond to me but could not ignore the baby's demand. Perhaps she needed to burp. Judith placed Emma over her shoulder and murmured softly, "Yes, yes darling, it's okay." But the baby kept arching her back, whimpering. So Judith sat her up on her lap, holding the little chin with one hand and patting the back with the other.

"She probably just needs to burp," I said, knowing there was no point in continuing the discussion until Emma quieted down. Finally she burped and drooled a line of sour milk bubbles onto her nightie, and Judith put her on the other breast.

"My father too," Judith said, her attention released again, and then—for a symbolic vignette had just been drawn for us—suddenly she smiled.

"Well, he was like Emma in a way, like an infant. It's that same quality of absoluteness. If you agree to give to me, he seemed to say, you must give everything. No halfhearted attention will do, not even to my small needs. Give to me! I want you totally. And if I responded to him at all, it was like I do now with the children, with total attention. Energy is drained from everything, but *everything*, else. They devour you. When I was a little girl I went through cycles; for a long period I would give to him, even when he wasn't at home. I gave to him, thinking about him, planning—it may sound silly, but it's true —planning the construction of complicated sentences I would use at dinner so he would praise me."

But it didn't seem silly at all. There were times when I had worn an outfit to school I knew my father would dislike—maybe the tights had runs in them, or the sweater was too tight. Anyway I knew he would see me as a disappointment, not up to the caliber of my mother. So before he came home I would change. I wore the clothes that were in style to school, but before dinner I would put on something neat that he would prefer, and then wrinkle it up a bit so he would think I had it on all day. There were times when I would purposely disappoint him—not sweep the floor after doing the dishes, or take a political position I knew would offend him. Other times I devoted my life to searching for the small gestures or qualities that would make him proud, but always, it was *him.* He presided over my inner life. And I could find no privacy.

I was amazed as I realized it, amazed that it was true, and utterly confused as to whether a certain kind of man devoured my attention in this way, or whether for a certain kind of man I offered myself up for devouring.

"And that's the price," finished Judith emphatically, as Emma, contented this time, let go of the nipple and lay back comfortably in her mother's arm, eyes half closed, mouth opened slightly, the milk dripping from its corner, a soft purr coming from her now. We stopped talking and smiled at her. One could never resist that infant purr of satiation, of perfect satisfaction.

Judith put the baby down again, and for a while we watched the rain and listened to the wind. It must be 3 A.M., I thought, and I dreaded how I would feel in the morning. Nevertheless, I could make no move to go upstairs.

We had felt closest to our fathers. Partly this is what had drawn us together; we had become like our fathers. Then why had their acceptance always presented such a struggle? Never something assumed, as if one had the love by birthright, but always, on the contrary, something that had to be fought for, that seemed ephemeral, as if in a moment it could be whisked away. The paternal tests were always difficult, and when the judgment was negative, no other punishment was needed. The disapproval of that man was punishment enough.

What had he wanted me to become? Like his own mother, unflinchingly maternal, sacrificial, unerringly attendant? Or like his wife, energetic, dignified, in control? I had tried, impossibly, to be both these women at once, ending up able to be neither with complete correctness, finally losing track of who I was underneath the heroic parts I played.

What he had gotten from me was complete dedication. Then it must have been I who had learned to be wary; I who, along with the facility of sensing what was asked of me, who for years complied, attended, bent down; I who slowly learned to be afraid. And now this fear, which was based not on a false anxiety but on a true assessment of my situation, this fear had burst into consciousness. It surrounded me with a protective seclusion, at times making me seem callous.

What I had done was to marry someone much more like my mother than my father. That paternal authority, that patriarchal benefactor, was at once too engulfing in his passion and too annihilating in his judgment to be allowed into one's bedroom in the flesh. Beneath my inherited devotion to the worlds of intellect, philosophical abstraction, and committed ideology, I sought—because I desperately needed—mothering.

As I watched Judith stroke Emma's thin, black baby hair, I realized something with a clarity and definition that opened up a wide, disturbing, inner channel of truth: if my boys had been girls I might not have feared losing myself in them nor resented giving to them in quite the same way.

It seems a small insight, perhaps. But the question: does it matter if you have a daughter or a son?—is one that parents tend to answer with a too-automatic no, denying that either sex might suffer some actual diminishment as a result of the parent's history. For years, the possibility that my attitudes toward a male or female child might involve an important difference seemed crass to me, too extreme, the flash of an unpleasant truth too sudden to accept. And yet this sort of greater ease with a child of one sex must be universal, indivisible from the fact that, up to now, our ways of loving have been so bound up with sexual roles. There is a simplicity of relationship that I feel with little girls that entangles itself into a burdensome complexity with boys. There is a simplicity of relationship—a security and confident separateness—that I feel with women that I can never hold on to for long with a man.

2

My son lies on a wide mattress, sleeping next to his friend. I try to read, listen to the rain whose wet, damp, sensuous odor pours through my window. Then I look up, see them lying there next to each other, each face bearing the singular, incomparable loveliness of a child asleep. Are those the same boys who, an hour ago, when two actors on TV began to kiss passionately, mocked vomiting and screamed—ooooh, gross—the two boys whom I overheard before talking about *tits*, big ones and little ones? They lie next to each other—their small faces utterly relaxed; their expressions, which so often during the day seek a tough manliness, a posture to which they devotedly and passionately aspire, are now utterly relinquished to vulnerability.

It is quiet in here. One light is on. The boys are turned toward each other. On the patterned quilt I have covered them with, their fingers rest as gracefully as any ballerina's.

Soon the mother of my son's friend comes to take him home. Although he is eight years old and she is a small woman, she picks him up, holds him comfortably, not wanting to jar him into a late-night, disorienting wakefulness. She smooths his hair. She whispers, Poor baby. And his long legs dangling downward almost to her own feet, she carries him downstairs.

At nine, my son is almost my own height, and so I cannot carry him to his bed, though at that moment I wish I could. But I walk him into the room, holding him against me so that he can lean as much as he likes, and lift him, at least partially, into bed. Then I go over to the other bed to cover his brother.

How can I describe in words the impression of vulnerability, the sense of his gentleness, that overpowers me whenever I see this second child asleep? His mouth rests slightly opened; his eyes relax into a smoothness so that they appear as two slanted black lines—the curve of his lashes. His light brown hair, which has never made up its mind to be curly or straight but instead insists on everything—kinky in front, straight on top, curly down the back and sides, tangles itself in disarray. It will be knotty in the morning. I don't know why I swallow tears each time I see him asleep, why I am possessed by fears that some extreme fragility will bring him harm someday, why he seems in every way so much less protected than his brother. I don't know if I project my own fears upon this child—some people think him sturdy, tenacious, a fighter —or if I see into a depth of him, and the frightened, easily wounded core that exists there. I suppose both images are true. But when I feel that wordless reaching out in him, when I sense the sudden terror that can overcome him in the face of failure of any kind, when I see the way failure makes him fold, fall, run away—usually he runs headlong into his room and returns covered from head to foot by a blanket—a failed reader, perhaps, or a failed writer of numbers over twenty, safely hidden now in his tent. When I see him hide that way, I glimpse more than an impression of the caves in which I hide from the judgment of the world.

He is only six. But he seems separate from me in a way his older brother never does. Two contradictory theories of child development lie side by side in my brain. One: the mother, through her being, her actions, her deepest feelings, her environment, creates the child; two: the child comes to us already himself or herself, we only hold them temporarily. Most modern thinkers subscribe to the first. Most cultures of the world to the second. People who are not parents subscribe to the first. But every parent I know gives a respectful nod to the second. It is a vision of our powerlessness that the second child brings.

Perhaps for this reason, I am able to have certain thoughts about him that I would never have allowed myself to experience with his brother.

When he lies on the floor at night, drawing or watching TV, quiet as he often is when he is alone, dressed in one of the long nightshirts he likes to wear around the house so that the elastic of his pajama pants won't hurt his stomach, I am acutely conscious of my desire to feminize him, to protect him from masculinity, to keep him from moving out of my world. Only rarely do I give in to this subversive urge—I have a fear of his losing his bearing altogether; that without *masculinity* in its most conventional sense, at least a part of it, he will falter, stay so close to me that he will not be able to walk away at all. Now he is passionate about dolls and cooking, delicate drawings, flowers and imaginary stories about winged swans who carry little boys to magical lands above the clouds and bring them home in time for dinner. It is not some pristine movement toward his psychic and physiological destiny that I watch drive him into that other male world, but the desire to be like his father and his brother, to find a meeting ground, to translate the natural and interior sense of his masculinity into external and easily accessible terms.

Determined that he be strong enough to negotiate the world (that ancient maternal betrayal), I may encourage his growing involvement in baseball which he clearly appropriates from his brother and friends without any authentic interest of his own, appropriates because he yearns to be a boy, too, to be a man. I may even buy him a toy gun if he begs me enough. Still, I am aware of the urge, the desire, to keep him tied to my world, and I wonder what sort of human being would result from the shameless determination on the part of a mother to feminize her son.

I expected all along that by the time I reached this point—the time to speak of my sons—I would experience a crescendo of understanding, that I would know what I want for them, that I would have clarified for myself some new relation of woman to boy which would some day find its glorious apotheosis in her manhood: Man to Woman.

I try to recall how the world felt to me when I was as old as my boys. When I was five my sister had recently been born and my father was discovering that he preferred, in certain ways, blond girls who resembled him, to dark-haired replicas of his somewhat mysterious and unattainable wife—no matter what their potential for comprehending Marxist philosophy and economics. When I was nine I was beginning to transform the real-life memories of my mother into the myths and images that would haunt my dreams for years, then shred and tear at the seams as I struggled to take them carefully apart, then reconstruct themselves into what seemed a more realistic pattern, only to assume mythical proportions once again in the form of the men whose temperaments would be so mysteriously attractive to me, tantalizingly familiar.

First James with his aloof but consistent protection. Then David with all his passionate need.

How do I integrate it all for my two boys? I want them to become men who are firmly grounded in their sexuality. I would like them to be proud lovers. I would like as much, however, for them to be seekers of emotional truth, anxious to nurture those they love, familiar with the connections between mind and body.

I wish them to catch the feelings that fly through the mind unarticulated and to develop the ability to use consciousness to give those feelings sense and clarity. Can they be delicate and powerful in their sex and also be like women?

My nine-year-old son is very much a boy, and he reminds me continually of how inevitably the world pushes in on us. The "things boys do," the desire to be like his father, the television, the school—all create him, take him from me, for good and for bad. And now this child whose features match mine line for line is thought by most to resemble his father. It is the gesture, the way of moving a hand to make a point, the shift and grace of the ass and thigh when he runs, the movement of the face in sadness, the closing of the face in fear, the way of life that begins to match James.

My father taught me as a political truth that there is no such thing as individual success or failure in the world of economics cut off from the system in which one flourishes or dies. It is the same with sexual development. It is true, as Dorothy Dinnerstein asserts, that the universal pattern of exclusive mother-raising creates insurmountable breaches for both boys and girls in the development of their sexual selves. But I cannot change that pattern alone. And if there is no one else to raise my children, no one else to attend to their emotional needs, I will certainly step in. The purely personal establishes itself like a cell-block around people, distorting the truths of our parenthood and of our sex. And it is a limitation, a distortion which is pathological in its inaccuracy, whose effect is criminal in its destructiveness.

When my older son was in the first grade I bought him a pair of handsome blue tights to keep out the February cold. Once he made the mistake of undressing for gym with the other boys on a day when he was wearing tights, and he was mocked. Only girls wear tights, they said. He, they continued absurdly, pointing at him, was a girl. He was humiliated. His sex, like anyone's, is a central foundation of his sense of himself. But there is more. To be called a girl, if you are a boy, is still far worse than the opposite. There is a relinquishing of power involved, a stepping down. No less in a child's world than in our own.

Our family lives in a neighborhood that is famous for its racial, political, cultural, and stylistic complexity. And yet, on the whole, in the neighborhood school for example, except for a smattering of families whom we know, sex roles are defined as rigidly, sexual politics are obeyed as unquestioningly, as when I was in elementary school almost thirty years ago. The boys play ball, develop strength and knowledge of their bodies and gain the incomparable confidence that accompanies that strength and knowledge. The girls, on the whole, do not. The girls talk endlessly and daily about their feelings and their lives. When my son tried to join one of those conversations he was informed that boys do not talk about those things.

He no longer wears tights to school on gym days. When he does, he puts socks over them so they will not be visible when his pants leg is raised.

But it is an illusion to think that our liberated criteria for dressing are comfort and practicality alone. It is comfortable and practical in the spring when the weather is turning warm, for example, to wear short jersey dresses over tights as much as to wear heavy dungarees. But I cannot imagine allowing my younger boy at five years old to go outside in a light, loose dress, though he used to ask me repeatedly to let him do just that. Instead I protect him from humiliation in a world which is waiting for him beyond the security of my embrace, beyond the certainty of my convictions.

The older one is growing away from me. And once again I find myself a failer of psychological tests. I cannot seem to stop this almost physiological sense of continued connection to him, this persistent identification, this boundary confusion. And yet, more and more he reminds me of the boys I grew up with, from whom I felt slightly estranged. Daily he loses that sense of bisexual possibility both his body and his mind possessed until about the age of five or six. When he flirts, loves, turns his attention away from me, I am not only proud of his autonomy and appropriate psychosexual development, skillful artisan of motherhood viewing her evident success with pride; I am also jealous, betrayed. I cannot forget the velvet softness of the small penis I was once allowed to stroke before I put on a freshly washed diaper.

He is so passionate about the Yankees that during the baseball season I begin to have obsessive fantasies about moving out of the house. I begin to dread the first moment of consciousness in the morning, when with my eyes only just opened, I will be accosted with newly learned batting averages or with some detail of Reggie Jackson's adolescence in which I cannot pretend the slightest interest, even in the pursuit of good motherhood.

The world waits for my sons, its long-established, collectively agreed upon definitions offering them a security, a fathomable identity, that I cannot hope to match alone. I watch the boyness of my children develop—in amazement at the power of culture, in fear of the price they will pay for their masculinity, and also in astonishment at their strength.

For there is another kind of moment, one in which I see that growing boyness as rich, worthy of emulation, one which recalls to me the envy I felt as a little girl of the powerful grace and agility, the various kinds of discipline, that seemed to me then to come along, as if unbidden, with even a childish masculinity.

The other day I watched my nine-year-old boy drown a certain sorrow on the shortstop line of a community baseball game. His movements as he ran hard to catch the grounder were elegant. His eyes narrowed into an intense dark line, he bent to scoop up the ball in an efficient movement that reminded me of all the graceful boys I had ever watched picking up balls, heedless of the beating sun that always made me sweat into quitting, oblivious to the rising dust from the playing field, to the strain of muscles that would surely ache the next morning. In two cohesive movements, he threw the ball just in time to stop the guy at first. Then he reached up and pushed his cap slightly back on his head so that his face was a bit more open to the sun.

To have been a boy.

I lie next to James still not knowing if our internal separations of the past year will soon become a living separation—that odd kind of divorce in which two people who must share their lives forever through their mutual history and their connection to their children live in separate houses. We live on the edge of our feelings for each other, deciding to jump off the edge, but pulling back several steps each time just before we jump. We no longer fight much, resigned to each other's immutable differences. Shall we relax into this resignation and learn to call it a new, tolerable, more mature kind of love? Or shall we jump over the edge into certain loneliness, some new, only partially desired, sort of developing selfhood?

I live on the edge, obsessed with its sparse geography, blinded by its relentless sun under which I see everything all too clearly. I lie beside James each night, feeling our thighs touch, the same way I have done for twelve years, and I sense his slowly accumulating plans: where to go next in contrast to my own endless confusion. His ability to plan in the midst of pain is based on his ability to accept the hard facts of life without continually questioning the validity of those facts with yet another compulsive examination, muddying each newly acquired certainty with a consideration of its opposite. I move a few inches away from him. I can feel his boundaries establish themselves.

To have been a boy.

I have a friend who is struggling to live through a difficult period in his life. He is committed to a marriage which he knows denies an enormous part of himself. He stays, he says, because of young children, because of his shared history with a woman for whom he feels strong affection. Like James and me, he lives on the edge, placing one foot tentatively over into vast space and then, contemplating the long way down, pulling back a few steps before those final precarious rocks to a place where he can rest again.

While he pulls back he works very hard. Far into the night, he tells me. He concentrates, has no trouble focusing on his very demanding, self-generating work. He produces scholarly paper after paper; he builds up accomplishments which several months from now will gain him well-deserved recognition, which in turn will reinforce that precious sense of who he is. The next time it will be a somewhat stronger man who walks to the edge. He works late into the night. He produces papers. The lonelier and more confused he is in his personal life, the harder he works. Work gives both immediate solace and long-range therapeutic change. He builds his muscles as my son does on the baseball field, with graceful movements he has picked up from the hundreds of men he has watched along the way. When he greets a welcomed fatigue at the end of the day, welcomed because the hard work has pushed his personal problems for the moment into a more acceptable perspective, he may raise his eyes to the evening sky in the same movement I saw in my son that afternoon.

To have been a boy.

Do you still feel sad about that other thing? I asked my son after the game.

Yes, he answered me in a voice calmed by exertion. But I'm not really worried about it right at the moment.

There was a time when I would have derided the masculine capacity to distance oneself through various kinds of work. And I still clearly see its danger when it is used to negate all consciousness of internal life, when it is used successfully to bury every vulnerability, every explosion of ambiguity or ambivalence. But if it is used to assure oneself that there is a life that persists beyond personal passions and emotional needs, that there are needs for things other than love that can sustain a person through inevitable hard times, then to reject this capacity is to flee from growth.

I have lived for over a year on the edge, refusing to step back and rest, not even looking up or around me for fear of losing sight of the reality of my despair. And the habits of autonomy, which I had thought I had so irreversibly developed, which might have been used to step one way or another off the edge, have languished instead.

Everything I am now involved in takes a great deal of time. The buildup of re-created habits: of work and of physical control. Habits of manhood that I want to own.

I was raised through my early years by a series of inattentive female housekeepers and by a man. My mother worked, supported the family. I remember her only in an occasional detail, rising Saturday morning at

noon, taking a cinder out of my eye, occasionally allowing me to bathe with her at night after she returned from
the office. So I do not know what in the way of conventional womanly maternity I offer my sons. I don't seem to
possess those feminine instincts usually assumed to be an
integral part of physiological womanhood. I don't have
certain of the conventional masculine strengths, but then
neither did my father. I would like my sons to be part
man, part woman. And whether they feel their sexuality
aroused and fired into a confusing, enriching inner explosion by other men or by women, I would like their sense
of being masculine to feel self-evident, nothing to do with
anything except that their bodies are molded in a certain
lovely way. The rest is for discovery and self-creation.

And yet, the moment I feel or say or write anything
about my sons, I am reminded that there is a world out
there. Because I am a woman in that world, I am incapable of giving them certain things that only their father
can give them.

Boys, naturally, led by the image of their bodies, will
want to be men. They will want to be men like the men
they know best. If their fathers are unable to give them
the possibility of a new, more maternal sort of manhood,
these boys, like generations of boys before them, simply
will not possess the qualities that most women I know,
including myself, yearn for, search for, demand, even beg
for in a man.

7
The Shameless Hussy

"You knew from her birth that she would be taken," my
father answered. "We'll have to harvest potatoes without
her help this year," my mother said, and they turned away
toward the fields, straw baskets in their arms. The water
shook and became just water again. "Mama. Papa," I called,
but they were in the valley and could not hear me.
— Maxine Hong Kingston,
*The Woman Warrior: Memoirs of a Girlhood
Among Ghosts*

One of the most widespread, persistent myths found
in cultures throughout the world is the myth of the Trickster. In a study of that myth, Paul Radin, an American
anthropologist, described him as Creator and Destroyer,
giver and negator. He wills nothing consciously, yet all
potential assertion lies within his energies. He is continually overwhelmed by passion and appetites, yet through
his life values come into being. He is Earthmaker, Creator
of the Universe, and then suddenly he is transformed into
a grotesque clown with genitals the size of mountains, or
he is turning the gold of some unsuspecting village elder
into a pile of shit. Both sacred and profane, characterized
by unsynthesized oppositions, he is the energetic and nat-

ural underside of the individual made collective, external, and accessible.

The Shameless Hussy is in some ways a personal equivalent of the Trickster. She is the bad-me turned whole. She acknowledges Lily Briscoe, understands the terrible temptation at the heart of her refusal of love; she grows until she glimpses the wisdom and autonomy of Hester Prynne, until she is no longer disembodied, no longer merely an aspect of myself. The trouble with the Shameless Hussy is that, once she is let out, it is not so easy to bury her again, no matter how inconvenient or disruptive her persistent consciousness may be. She is no weakling. On the contrary, she embodies some of the most powerful forces I know.

> Telling the truth about one's body: a necessary, freeing subject for a woman writer.
> —Tillie Olsen, *Silences*

Long before I knew the word *masturbate*, my sister and I used to "think of naked"—sometimes together (each telling a story which would ensure the other's arousal) and sometimes alone. I always knew when she had done it because she would fall asleep with her underpants still down at her knees. I never wore underpants at night so no one could tell. But sometimes during the day, in the middle of a geometry or a history lesson at school for example, I would hear the sudden command in my brain: *Jump up on the chair and yell, I think of Naked!* Terrified of that devilish, willful, shameless part of myself I would say, bargaining: I will not yell that, but I will write it in my notebook in large letters, risking exposure: I THINK OF NAKED. I will wait for sixty seconds with my hands in my lap. If no one sees, then I may cross it out or crumple up the paper and stuff it in my pocket to be taken out at home when I am alone and destroyed with a sigh of relief: I have escaped again.

Occasionally the desire to escape was overcome, without consciousness or will, by the desire to expose the secret once and for all, to say it all out loud, the worst of it, to fling it in the face of the world. We used to have a rule in our house once we grew into teenagers that when you were having your period, you had to wrap the used Kotex up in a brown paper bag and throw it immediately into the incinerator. Just putting it in the bathroom trash basket was not allowed. We had to get rid of the smell. One day, innocently opening my bag lunch in the school cafeteria, in expectation of the tuna fish with chopped celery, the tangerine, the Devil Dog I had packed so carefully that morning, I found instead my bloody Kotex. I had, of course, dumped my lunch into the incinerator and taken the other brown bag to school. An innocent mistake, perhaps. But it has assumed symbolic importance for me if only on the evidence that it has remained in my mind so long. No one caught me. I saw the contents of the bag before pulling it out and then just threw it surreptitiously and quietly away. What has remained in my consciousness must be the secret desire to reveal the bloody Kotex to the world.

It is neither cavalier nor a question of personal pathology, this compulsion in women writers, in women in general, to say what has been the unsayable, to write and speak of the bloody Kotex, the joy of masturbation, the incestuous desire, the feeling of submissive abandon or of a paralyzing, dry indifference during sex.

A married woman, out of an only partially despised sense of loyalty, talks infrequently to her women friends about the sexual problems she continues to have with her husband. He has convinced her of his right to privacy. She thinks perhaps he is right. The inescapable implication of any love is loyalty. Then, in predictable cycles, she spills out the truth, tells and retells the painful details of their long-suffered sexual breach, the way they can never seem to meet up with each other for long. The private realm has been the realm of women's oppression, and we have been alienated from our own vision of the truth in the name of privacy, making an inexorable link between confession and freedom.

Still, how can it be borne? The humiliation of releasing the secret?

I might not have been able to reveal even the little that is here if my father were alive. And now, among the fears that threaten to silence me, a central one is that my sons, reading this book one day, will be ashamed, will judge.

It ought to be a simple and evident truth, one not requiring a great deal of analytical time and attention, the idea that one's body encloses oneself, that there is a deep, not always apparent, relation between body feelings, emotional needs, and intellectual passions; that it is therefore essential to explore each realm with a fullness unlimited by conventional expectation: "telling the truth about one's body . . ."

This year, for the first time in my life, I have pursued physical exercise with all the passion and commitment with which I have for years pursued the clarification of the layers of my mind. I joined a neighborhood gym.

I review my numerous volumes of journals, kept now for fifteen years. Every few pages, I read: I must get my body into shape, assume control over its life. But there is no record in all those years of the accomplishment of this repeated promise to myself.

This year I began to fulfill the promise. What enabled me to do so was talking back to my father; standing separate from James; being loved by David; being abandoned by David; disobeying my father by publicizing the unacceptable core; holding and caressing the lithe, magical body of a five-year-old boy; watching a nine-year-old boy bend ever so gracefully to catch a grounder; seeing a two-year-old girl climb a mountain of sand and mud; holding and cherishing the mother of the two-year-old girl, seeking her arms for my shoulders, rounded in defeat, her hand on my hair, her unwavering support and belief in me when I felt abandoned by all the world.

She dreamed I was lost in a cave. She found my father and made him move the boulder so that she could come in and get me out. But I refused to emerge. So she dreamed it again until I agreed.

The first day I went to the gym I was sweating with fear. I put on my leotard and pretended blindness when I passed the scale.

"Do you wish to weigh yourself?" the supercilious young male attendant said.

I simply stared at him, his question itself an unspeakable infraction. I was shown the weightlifting machines. I was given a schedule of calisthenics classes. They asked me to do push-ups and sit-ups and leg-ups and jumping-jacks, to test my capacity for tolerating stress. They thought my heart was beating that fast because I was physically tired. I was terrified and humiliated. They had a fat-measurer—an object that looked like a long, dull tweezer and that was used to measure the fat at the waist, on the thigh, on the upper arm. They measured the inches of my breasts, my waist, my hips, my thighs. I thought I must have gotten caught in a nightmare. The young attendant said, "Do some chins." And he pointed to some steps leading up to an iron bar.

"I can't do even one chin," I confessed, looking down. He smirked. He wrote something down on his pad.

"Go and weigh yourself and tell me the truth," he said next. "You'll be kidding no one but yourself."

I went to the scale, noted my weight and informed him, deducting five pounds without consideration. It was the only kind of rebellion I had allowed myself.

I fled to the pool, the water, where I would feel comfortable, serene, light, graceful, adept. The pool was surrounded by floor-to-ceiling mirrors. I saw twelve reflections of myself immediately and three more when I neared the diving edge. I was crying. I was determined. I swam, hiding myself in the water, exhausting my brain with the demand for physical precision.

I left the gym, went home, and cried for an hour. Then I washed my hair and called to complain about the impudent young man.

After several weeks I had learned some startling things.

—The impudent young man was indeed impudent and condescending, but he was also not much more than a boy, a conceited, posturing, self-aggrandizing, silly, performing young boy. I was amazed at his power to terrify me.

—There was another young man who worked at the gym, about the same age as the first, a young Italian man from Brooklyn who worked part-time as a gym teacher in junior high school, part-time in this gymnasium, and on weekends at the post office carting heavy mail. He worked out passionately and led the calisthenics classes. He told me he always wore heavy blue sweat pants because he was ashamed of his skinny legs. He smiled so sweetly at me and so regularly that I began to attend his classes as much for the pleasant sexual arousal I felt in his presence as for the commitment to getting in shape and losing weight. I began to feel so comfortable with him that I allowed him to teach me how to use the weightlifting machines, which I have come to respect instead of automatically hate.

—The machines are pure in a way. Finite. And manageable. They demystify the tremendous aura of intimidation which has always surrounded the life of the body for me. You lift or push only as much weight as is tolerable. You move slowly and for a specified number of times. Completing the whole cycle of machines takes less than half an hour, and if you work out on the machines three times a week, you begin to notice new lines in your shoulders, a hardness in your thighs, a straightness to your posture that was not there before. You can't help noticing that you lift as many weights as many of the men, and so you are less afraid on the streets. Finiteness. Predictability. Demystification. Control. My body is subject to my desire and expresses my desire.

—I love the gym now. I still hate the endless floor-to-ceiling mirrors and the scales computerized into a perfect accuracy.

—I love the locker room where women of every shape and age and size walk around naked, drying their hair, talking casually to other women. They are often overheard confessing their initial terrors of the gym. The dancers and the athletes and the stewardesses, whose bodies are tight and gorgeous and smooth, are usually very helpful in these discussions to the teachers and the writers and the mothers of newborn infants. They have helped me a great deal.

My body has felt both glorious and alien to me. I have felt a man's hand move in me with such an adept grace that my consciousness was, for the moment, embodied utterly within my vagina, was safely enclosed by it, and all the world, for that moment, floated around me as its center in a rhythmical pattern of perfect comprehensibility. I have held a man, felt him inside me, with such a total strangeness, swallowing such feelings of hatred and rage, that I have floated far away, beyond the shrieking white of the ceiling into the black sky, and I have hovered there staring down at my alien body, hating it for its submission, for its ability to completely ignore the truths I knew with my mind.

I have watched myself in a dozen mirrors at the gym, thinking, there is a body, a body like any other, a human form, graceful there, out of shape there, but ordinary, real, beautiful. If I care for it I can make it the way I wish it to be. I have sat on the edge of the pool, my thighs pulled into my stomach and breasts, hiding myself, my arms around my thighs, holding myself and hiding myself with the same gesture because I was completely convinced of my vast ugliness, my immediately apparent lack of grace.

My body is a sometimes inconvenient, but indisputable expression of my feeling, my thought, my situation in life.

My sexuality, like the physical development at the gym, is something I want to learn more about. Like the Trickster, it can be Creator and Destroyer—but not destroyer of male potency and adult masculinity, and not the creator of perfect life. Creator and destroyer, alternately, and as yet without integration, of my autonomy, of my ability to know that I exist quite alone, without being visualized by another.

I have been unhinged and rendered groundless by the power and force of sex, and for me, thus far, this has happened with men. Unhappily, the sense of groundlessness, which can be creative if I ultimately claim my ground again (as happened to me after the long crisis of new motherhood) has not always functioned to my benefit and toward my growth in loving men. But I would feel myself to be a fraud in the extreme if I were now to assert that the ultimate responsibility of that loss of self belongs to the men, even though their fears of intimacy have hurt and disappointed me again and again.

One male friend says that each time he meets a woman with whom he might share a great deal of himself, he retreats in fear—into his work or into a rejuvenated hope that he will be able to patch together a marriage that he left five years ago because he and his wife, mother of his children, have absolutely no emotional, sexual, or intellectual meeting ground.

Another man, also a friend, speaks to me in long and close conversations about the work we share and the fears of inadequacy in general to which we are both subject. But whenever I try to reveal to him the specific facts of my personal life, or to probe his, he quiets me very quickly with a tone, a harsh movement, a change of subject.

"I have only one life," a woman said in a workshop at a women's conference I attended. She was tall, a beautiful woman, between forty and fifty. Her hair was black, thick, brushed simply back from her forehead, yet she possessed an air of exotic sensuality.

She spoke without melodrama, straightforwardly: "There are times when, thanks to my ideals, I am without a man for long periods of time. I am no hypocrite, I am a free woman," she said ironically. "But I am lonely. I want love in my life, and for me, that means a man. I want an abiding friendship. A lover. I want a lover I can trust. I find only little boys who run away. If I cannot find a lover I can trust, I will take a little boy who runs away."

And yet, it is not only men who are confused. Here are the words of Maxine Hong Kingston, author and hero of *The Woman Warrior*:

> Marriage and childbirth strengthen the swords-woman, who is not a maid like Joan of Arc. Do the women's work; then do more work, which will become ours too. No husband of mine will say, "I could have been a drummer, but I had to think about the wife and the kids. You know how it is." Nobody supports me at the expense of his own adventure. Then I get bitter: no one supports me; I am not loved enough to be supported. That I am not a burden has to compensate for the sad envy when I look at women loved enough to be supported. Even now, China wraps double binds around my feet.

I was preparing myself to live alone. I heard of a family buying a new washing machine and dryer. That night I walked the streets of my neighborhood for several hours, crying, thinking: Can I be so jealous of a washing machine?—imagining my cremated father turning over in his appropriately nonmaterial grave. It was not precisely the washing machine, but the ease of being supported, the washing machines, and the cars, and the maids, and the country houses. The past shines attractively, glowing with a false simplicity. *Then* (I allow myself to think), then I was happy. Knew my place. I created a home. Not plagued by dreams of excellence and ambitions of power, I locked my eyes upon the road just before me; my hands were filled with the hands of my children. And the man? I allowed him to go into the world, unhampered by my bitterness, and in return he looked upon me with gratitude. I meant peace to him. I was good.

But now I am a troublemaker. I scream his duties after him as he drags his body off to work, his body which is marked by exhaustion, the exhaustion of work, of changing, as tired as mine. What is the source of my remarkable pride in this troublemaking woman I have become, led only by the uncertainty of her own vision?

These are details, perhaps, small and momentary, even peripheral impressions that collect in a life. And yet the peripheral impressions of passionate women wanting more from distant men, and of emotional men retreating from strong connections of various kinds to women and seeking a colder, more distant partner, are impressions which gather and coalesce into an undeniably central reality. When stories of many women's lives are layered closely together, stories of transitory passion, confessions of marital breaches, the rarity of intimate friendship between an occasional man and woman, the sound of a trapdoor is heard undeniably closing.

Like Lily Briscoe I have to admit, with a great sense of loss, that up to now strong connection to a man has undermined me, dissipated my energy, left me confused as to the validity of the most personal aspects of my vision of the world. That is something for which I can hold no one else responsible. The vulnerability is mine. It is not in an attempt to dissipate responsibility, then, but only in an attempt to understand origins and the ways in which the persistent force of those origins affect my life, that again and again, wanting to or not, I return to my father.

I have thought a lot recently about incest. I have noticed that when you have loved a man for a long time, lived together for years the way you once did with your parents, he assumes certain familial qualities. Sometimes making love to James, I feel my father, various loved uncles and cousins, all lined up near my bed as if waiting in turn to inhabit the body beside me. If their kinship derived its meaning and fearsomeness from long association and intimate mutual knowledge, then certainly this man is kin too. Sometimes, I close my eyes and pretend he is a stranger, a less familiar friend and far less dear, or shortly my father may jump into the bed with us, crawling into my lover's body and extinguishing my passion.

What can the analytic thinkers mean when they speak of an "unresolved" oedipal complex? If a resolved one means that a heterosexual woman is free to enjoy sex with men who are essentially kind and truly passionate, then mine is at least somewhat resolved. But if it means that the chains of memory are unlinked, that the infantile time when my parents' bodies were the only source of passion for me has somehow been dislodged from my erotic life and sent to drift away, then I don't understand resolution, and I certainly don't claim it.

I can allow myself these words and thoughts since my father is dead. If he were alive, he would be outraged. Reading this he would turn his head to the side and say with expressive distaste, *Oh, for God's sake*, or just utter some guttural sound of disgust mixed with a moan and a sigh. The moan would mean he was having to tolerate my extremism again. He would be embarrassed that this life-long inability to separate the Dignified from the Undignified and set the second in a securely private place appears to be so unextinguishable an aspect of my character. The sigh would be a tribute to his finally accepted impotence in changing me. When he sighed like that, I glimpsed the best of the man. I know he saw me as a rather clumsy hero, awkward and often inaccurate, but determined to reproduce the images inside my head which so insistently demanded attention. I, at least, have learned, recalling that early forbidden desire to draw the painting of my mother, that I will find some close enough reflection on which to focus my vision if denied the accessibility of my first choice. And perhaps by looking across the room to the Indian mother and child—that pattern I developed out of necessity in childhood which I now recreate in writing—I find a reflection, its perspective just slightly askew, which comes even closer than I had hoped to apprehending a facet of reality itself.

When I think I have succeeded, I am as likely as my father was to try to convert the people I love, the students I teach, the friends I treasure—the world. And I hope I can fail as he did, with increasing clarity and diminishing shame.

I wasn't able to bring my mother back to life by drawing her picture over and over again. But I can write my past into a tentative comprehension. And I can glimpse a new direction in a closing page.

Bibliography

Obviously this is not a scholarly work in the traditional sense. But it has been the sort of book that required a great deal of reading—for purposes of clarification of ideas, of knowing what had been said before, and for the sustaining of the courage that is required to write autobiography when it involves a true revelation of the self. I have a deep respect for those women writers who use the self in the writing of fiction and nonfiction and who do so because they cannot do otherwise. I would like to mention, therefore, the books which have been most important to me in the writing of this book, the works which have given me knowledge, or insight, or confidence, in the hope that others will read them and use them, and in a recognition of the women whose ideas and self-awareness gave birth to mine.

Bengis, Ingrid. *Combat in the Erogenous Zone.* New York: Alfred A. Knopf, 1972.
Cook, Blanche Weisen, ed. *Crystal Eastman on Women and Revolution.* New York: Oxford University Press, 1978.
De Beauvoir, Simone. *The Second Sex.* New York: Vintage Books, 1974.

Didion, Joan. *Slouching Towards Bethlehem.* New York: Farrar, Straus & Giroux, 1968.

Dinnerstein, Dorothy. *The Mermaid and the Minotaur.* New York: Harper & Row, 1976.

Drabble, Margaret. *The Waterfall.* New York: Popular Library, 1977.

Gordon, Mary. *Final Payments.* New York: Random House, 1978.

Gornick, Vivian. "Female Narcissism as a Metaphor in Literature," in *Essays in Feminism.* New York: Harper & Row, 1978.

————. *In Search of Ali Mahmoud.* New York: Saturday Review Press/E. P. Dutton, 1973.

Griffin, Susan. *Woman and Nature.* New York: Harper & Row, 1978.

Johnson, Joyce. *Bad Connections.* New York: G. P. Putnam's Sons, 1978.

Kingston, Maxine Hong. *The Woman Warrior: Memoirs of a Girlhood Among Ghosts.* New York: Alfred A. Knopf, 1976.

Konecky, Edith. *Allegra Maud Goldman.* New York: Harper & Row, 1976.

Lessing, Doris. "An Unposted Loveletter," in *Stories.* New York: Alfred A. Knopf, 1978.

McNeill, Elizabeth. *Nine and a Half Weeks.* New York: E. P. Dutton/Henry Robbins, 1978.

Moglen, Helene. *Charlotte Brontë: The Self Conceived.* New York: W. W. Norton, 1978.

Olsen, Tillie. *Silences.* New York: Delacorte/Seymour Lawrence, 1978.

————. "I Stand Here Ironing" and "Tell Me A Riddle," in *Tell Me A Riddle.* New York: Dell, 1971.

Redinger, Ruby V. *George Eliot: The Emergent Self.* New York: Alfred A. Knopf, 1975.

Rich, Adrienne. *The Dream of a Common Language: Poems*

1974–1977. New York: W. W. Norton & Co., 1978.

———. *Of Woman Born.* New York: W. W. Norton & Co., 1976.

Rosenthal, Carole. "Fusion," "Inside, Outside," in *Love Stories by New Women*, Red Clay Press, anthologized in *Secrets* (Gallimaufry Press), and *Reasonable Creatures*, a novel in progress.

Rossner, Judith. *Attachments.* New York: Simon & Schuster, 1977.

Schor, Lynda. *Appetites.* New York: Warner Books, 1975.

———. *True Love and Real Romance.* New York: Coward McCann, 1979.

Sexton, Linda Gray and Ames, Lois, eds. *Anne Sexton: A Self-Portrait in Letters.* Boston: Houghton Mifflin, 1977.

Smith, Lilian, ed. Michelle Cliff. *The Winner Names the Age: A Collection of Writings.* New York: W. W. Norton & Co., 1978.

Ullman, Liv. *Changing.* New York: Alfred A. Knopf, 1977.

Woolf, Virginia. *To the Lighthouse.* New York: Harcourt, Brace & World, 1927.

———, ed. Jeanne Schulkind. *Moments of Being: Unpublished Autobiographical Writings.* New York: Harcourt Brace Jovanovich, 1978.